TEACHING CHARACTER

Teacher's Idea Book for Middle School Grades

Anne C. Dotson

&

Karen D. Dotson

TEACHING CHARACTER

TEACHER'S IDEA BOOK FOR MIDDLE SCHOOL GRADES

by Anne C. Dotson & Karen D. Dotson

Produced and published by
CHARACTER DEVELOPMENT GROUP

Character Development Group
PO Box 9211
Chapel Hill, NC 27515-9211

(919) 967–2110, fax (919) 967–2139

Cover design by Sandy Nordman Design

ISBN 0-9653163-4-3 $24.00

Acknowledgements

I would like to thank the following persons for their contributions to this work:

My best friend and husband, Ray, whose love, support, help and encouragement gave me the confidence to get out of the box, to do a paradigm shift, to grow and stretch.

My co-author, daughter, and friend, Karen, without whose expertise and encouragement this work would not have the quality it does, and her husband Gregory, who enthusiastically supported this project from its inception.

Jonathan and Joyce, for believing in us.

My principal, Cynthia Metzger, whose faith in my integrity and abilities gave me courage to try!

Contents

We must remember that intelligence is not enough. Intelligence plus character, that is the goal of true education.

—Martin Luther King, Jr.

Every piece of marble has a statue in it waiting to be released by someone of sufficient skills to chip away the unnecessary parts. Just as the sculpture is to marble, so is education to the soul. It releases it. For only the educated are free. You cannot create a statue by smashing the marble with a hammer, and you cannot by force of arms release the spirit of the soul.

—Confucius

Introduction

Teaching Character to Middle-School Students

To educate a person in mind and not in morals is to educate a menace to society.

—Theodore Roosevelt

Good character can be defined in cognitive, affective, and behavioral terms, but perhaps a simple way to define it is: knowing what is right and good, wanting what is right and good, and doing what is right and good. When we identify persons as having "good character," we are saying that they adhere to a set of behaviors and beliefs which our culture commonly holds as desirable. This unwritten code of good character transcends the many cultures that make up our society; in fact, such a code is necessary for us to live together peacefully.

There is no doubt that character can be taught. Indeed, most children learn character from their parents and other influential adults. By teaching character traits in school, we are emphasizing and repeating lessons being taught at home. And for students lacking a stable home environment, school-based character education can help teach what they may not learn otherwise. Our focus as educators is not only to teach subjects and facts, but to teach ways of being in the world, to teach methods for finding greater happiness and productivity as adults. Our reward is better educated students and better citizens.

This idea book has been compiled to help you educate your students both in mind and in character. The lessons are designed to be taught in just a few minutes per day and in any discipline. The ideas presented here are intended to function as a springboard for your own creativity. Please adapt them as needed to suit your subject, your school, and your students.

Finally, in teaching these materials you may have the opportunity—and the obligation—to apply the lessons to your own life. After all, we cannot teach what we do not know.

Responsible

Definition

> **Obliged or expected to account for**

Objective

Students will be able to identify tasks they are responsible for at home and at school.

Application to students' lives

A responsible student takes charge of himself or herself and accepts the consequences of his or her actions and words.

Learning to accept responsibility for books, supplies, and homework gets students off to a good start in the school year.

Students need to begin the year understanding that the attitude of "That's just the way I am" does not demonstrate responsibility.

RESPONSIBLE: *Obliged or expected to account for*

Short Lessons

- Write or review class rules and discuss each student's responsibility to abide by these rules.

- Brainstorm ways to demonstrate responsibility for school work. Have each student identify one area of responsibility they will work on.

- Discuss chores assigned at home. What are the consequences of not doing these chores? How many of the students have pets? Who is responsible for taking care of the pets?

- Discuss what responsibilities students think that parents have toward their children. Do those responsibilities change as children get older?

- Identify the responsibilities students have compared with other persons they live with, such as siblings. Does the baby of the family have the same responsibilities? Why or why not?

- Ask students, "What are the responsibilities you'd like to have as an adult? Why?" Have students write these responsibilities on paper and collect the papers. Ask volunteers to share their ideas.

- Have students choose a person they know, such as a policeman, nurse, teacher, principal, or fast food worker, then write down what they think that person's responsibilities are.

- Have students list at least 5 things they would expect their students to be responsible for if they were the teacher. Write all the ideas on the board and tally which five things got the greatest number of "votes."

- Ask students to identify the advantages of being responsible when they come to school. How do they benefit?

- Discuss with students how they plan to assume responsibility for their lunch cards or lunch money during the school year. (Other examples include coats, books, book bags, and pencils.)

- Talk about who is responsible for doing their laundry and cleaning their rooms. How can they assume responsibility for these tasks? What effect could it have if they take on responsibility for these things?

Enter your classroom every day looking for some way to make every student feel good about something. It may be the way a student is dressed, answers a question, helps another student, etc. Use any opportunity, anywhere, anytime.

—Joseph Katarski

Student Assignments

- Practice keeping a list of all homework this week. Note when you have completed each assignment.

- Organize your notebook or folder by subject area, and decide how you will keep track of each subject's materials.

- Ask your parent or guardian what their responsibilities are. As homework, write a paragraph describing those responsibilities.

- Assume a new responsibility at home, such as cooking dinner one night or taking care of a younger brother or sister or a neighbor's child for an hour. Write a paragraph about your responsibility and what it involves.

- Work in teams to design a poster demonstrating responsibility.

Bulletin Board Ideas

- Put "A responsible student brings…" at the top of a large bulletin board, and place a cut-out diagram of a student or students in the center of the board. Around the image of the student, put pictures of supplies that students need for class each day, such as pencil, paper, books, folders, and homework.

- Display students' posters showing how to demonstrate responsibility.

- Use a waiter-type character called "Mr. Responsible" holding a bottle with "Education" written on it. Out of the character's mouth have a balloon with the phrase, "It all depends on me." Use the heading, "Education served here."

- Dedicate a bulletin board to "Responsible Students of the Week." Take pictures or draw silhouettes of students and choose 2-3 each week for the spotlight. Look for opportunities to reinforce responsible behavior by putting students' pictures on the board.

NOTES

Self-Control

Definition

Controlling one's actions and responses

Objective

Students will be able to identify techniques for controlling anger, disciplining themselves, and doing the right thing. They will understand that proper diet and rest have an important role in self-control.

Application to students' lives

By learning strategies for making positive choices and for controlling angry feelings, students will be able to resist doing things that are not good for them or for others.

As students learn that they are responsible for their actions and reactions, classroom control will improve.

Self control is important to success in extra-curricular activities students are involved with, such as music, sports, cheerleading, drill team, and jobs.

SELF-CONTROL: *Controlling one's actions and responses*

Short Lessons

- Identify strategies for practicing self-control, such as: counting to 10, stopping to breathe deeply several times, going for a walk, thinking about the consequences, and trying to identify what the other person is feeling. Have students give examples of when they have used these strategies.

- Identify foods that represent healthy choices, and discuss how eating properly versus not eating well affects their behavior. Your students may not believe that it makes a difference. Ask them to track "how good they feel" and see if eating has any effect on them.

- Talk about the importance of eating breakfast. How many of your students skipped breakfast on this particular day? Stress the importance of breakfast to their mental capabilities.

- Discuss examples of persons who no longer have control over their lives. Ask the students how they would feel if they were in prison or confined to a bed. Help students identify the advantages of exercising control over emotions and actions.

- Talk about athletes and how they become good enough to get their million-dollar jobs. When top athletes have these good jobs, can they quit? What happens when athletes lose self-control? Point out that self-control is a learned skill, just as athletic training is learned.

- Define the qualities of "aggressive" and "assertive." Discuss ways to get your point across without being pushy or losing your control.

- Discuss verbal and non-verbal communication. Role-play situations in which non-verbal conflict causes problems, and discuss possible ways to control non-verbal reactions.

- Ask students to identify situations in which peer pressure could overwhelm self-control. Develop a list of the kinds of pressures your students face.

- Discuss how self-control is important in not submitting to peer pressure. Identify strategies for using self-control to overcome peer pressure. (Examples could include avoiding areas where students smoke or finding friends who have similar interests.)

- Talk about what students can do if they have not exercised self-control. Remind them that feeling angry at themselves is not a good strategy because it undermines their self-esteem. Do they ever punish themselves? Suggest that they think of ways to discipline themselves.

- Discuss the importance of good self-esteem for self-control. Help students understand that when they think well of themselves, it becomes easier to ask themselves to control their anger, eat healthy foods, or resist peer pressure.

The art of living consists in knowing which impulses to obey and which must be made to obey.
—Sydney J. Harris

Student Assignments

- Pay close attention to every situation today and write down all the times you see someone practicing self-control. What are the consequences?

- Pay attention to every situation today and write down all the times you see someone lose their self-control. What are the consequences?

- How many opportunities do you have in one day to practice self-control? What techniques do you use most often? Keep a list of both.

- Keep a log of your food choices for several days and record whether these choices affect how you feel.

- Write several paragraphs describing an incident in which you practiced self-control, and the outcome of that incident. Be sure to use introductory sentences and supporting evidence in each paragraph.

Bulletin Board Ideas

- Put a student figure on one side of the board and feet going across the width of the board. At the top, write "Step into tomorrow with" and at the bottom, "Self-control." On each of the feet going across the board, write techniques for self-control, such as "stop and think," "breathe deeply," "think before you react," "count to 10," "make wise food choices," and "consider the consequences."

- Display a door with a large doorknob. Use yellow paper to represent a "light" shining through the key hole and to spell out the words, "You are responsible for your actions and reactions." Use the header, "Self-control is the key to unlocking your potential."

- Show students in various peer-pressure situations, such as saying 'no' to smoking, studying for a test when others are talking, and sitting quietly in an assembly. Use the header, "What is popular is not always right, and what is right is not always popular."

- Display figures representing the principal's office, jail, hospital, police car, and parents looking angry. Use the header, "Control yourself or someone else will."

P u n c t u a l

Definition

On time, prompt

Objective

Students will learn the meaning of the word and demonstrate ways to be punctual. Students will apply the concept of punctuality beyond school events to include family outings, chores, and commitments to teams and clubs.

Application to students' lives

Being on time is a way to demonstrate dependability and is an essential part of keeping a job.

Punctuality is a common courtesy; in effect, not being punctual is stealing another person's time.

By evaluating their weekly schedules, students will understand that trying to do too many activities can make them constantly late.

PUNCTUAL: *On time, prompt*

Short Lessons

- Ask students to list school events that they depend on to occur "on time." Examples include the bell ringing at the end of class, lunch breaks, the school bus arriving as scheduled, and the end of the school year.

- Ask students to think of a wide range of situations in which promptness is needed. Examples include stores opening on time, TV programs beginning on time, and movies starting as scheduled.

- Give students a homework assignment that is not due for several days, and then discuss how they plan to be punctual with that assignment. When the assignment is due, talk about whether they planned ahead to get it completed on time.

- Discuss the advantages of taking care of homework assignments as soon as possible versus waiting until the last minute. Talk about how the approach they take can affect their stress.

- Ask students how they get themselves up in the morning. How many use alarm clocks? How many depend on a parent or sibling to wake them? What are the advantages and disadvantages of having their own clock to wake them up?

- Discuss how using a planner can help students evaluate when they are not allowing enough time for homework and proper rest.

- Review school rules for tardiness to school and to class. Stress the fact that late-comers to class miss important information and interrupt the learning in progress.

- Brainstorm a list of all the excuses people use for being late. What is the wildest excuse they have ever heard? Which ones have they used? Does anyone know a dog that eats homework?

- Discuss what happens when they are part of a group and someone makes the entire group late for an event. How do they feel about that person? Ask students to provide examples of when this has happened.

- Talk about strategies for being on time. Choose a hypothetical situation, such as being on time for school, and strategize ways to be punctual.

Don't put off for tomorrow what you can do today, because if you enjoy it today you can do it again tomorrow.

—James A. Michener

Student Assignments

- Be sure to write your assignments down in a daily planner. [Teachers: Look at each student's planner to see what they have recorded.]

- Write several sentences using the word 'punctual'; each sentence should demonstrate different effects of being punctual or not being punctual.

- Interview a manager at McDonald's, at a grocery store, or in your neighborhood. Ask the manager how important it is for employees to be on time and how it affects the business if employees are late. Write a paragraph about your interview.

- Keep a record for one week of all the events you attend, when the events are scheduled, and whether you are on time. (Events can include school, church or club events, TV programs you want to watch, or family outings.) Also, record when you are late because of the actions of someone else. How did it make you feel to have to wait?

- Estimate the number of times you look at a clock in one day. Then, keep a tally of the actual number of times you look to see what time it is in a given day. Also, record the number of different clocks you use in the day.

Bulletin Board Ideas

- Place a clock in the center of the board with the header, "Don't merely count your days—Make your days count."

- Draw a large videocamera or movie reel with film coming out of it. On the 'film,' have squares with the character traits that have already been taught. Be sure that "Punctual" is readily visible. At the top of the board, have the message: "Good habits to develop."

- Use a drawing of an umpire saying "Time Out!" Beside that, have a long list of assignments that a typical student might have, including school work and chores. At the bottom of the board, ask: "Ever feel like your TIME is OUT? Plan ahead."

- Draw a large star on the bulletin board, against dark background paper. Put every student's name or picture on the large star and add many smaller stars around the perimeter. Use the header, "Be punctual—Just like the stars."

NOTES

R e s p e c t

Definition

> To have high regard for, to hold in esteem, to treat with courtesy and consideration

Objective

Students will be able to apply the concept of respect to people, places and things.

Application to students' lives

Learning respect will help students develop a positive rapport with parents, teachers, and friends.

Respect for others will strengthen self-confidence by generating positive feedback.

Respecting others, including peers, will help reduce unkind words and 'put-downs' among the students.

RESPECT: *To have high regard for, to hold in esteem, to treat with courtesy and consideration*

Short Lessons

- Talk about how good manners (such as courtesy, politeness, and kindness) demonstrate respect. What actions demonstrate a lack of respect?

- Brainstorm ways in which we communicate verbally. Have students develop a list of positive and negative words they hear every day. Which words demonstrate respect? Which words are "put-downs"? How do these words make them feel?

- Describe how tolerance for other people demonstrates respect. How can we show appreciation for differences in our culture?

- Discuss rules. What are rules for? Why do we have rules? Which rules do we like? Are there rules we don't like? Relate this to playing a game, such as football. How does following the rules demonstrate respect?

- Using the U.S. flag, lead the class in the Pledge of Allegiance. Discuss how this demonstrates respect for our country. What is the correct position for reciting the pledge? How does this position demonstrate respect?

- Discuss pushing in lunch lines or cutting in front of others at movie theaters or at games. What are other ways students do not respect each other? Why would they push each other but not push an adult?

- Use money as an example of respect. Would we throw it in the trash? Why does money deserve respect?

- Ask students how they show respect for themselves. What does a person's way of walking, acting, and dressing say about him or her?

- Discuss personal property. What does it mean to respect someone else's property? How do they feel when someone messes with their stuff?

- Ask students how they can show respect to their parents and grandparents. Why should we respect older people?

The secret of education is respecting the pupil.

—Ralph Waldo Emerson

Student Assignments

- Be spies. Pay attention and try to catch other students or teachers being respectful. Nominate these people for a ribbon in school colors to wear for the week. [Teachers: Allow students to present the person with a "respect ribbon."]

- Keep a respect log. For 24 hours, list every example you can find of people demonstrating respect. This list could include family members, strangers on the bus, or a clerk at the neighborhood store. As a class, list how many different ways there are to show respect.

- Practice thinking, "I am respectful when…" in every conflict you find yourself during the day. Be prepared to share with the class tomorrow.

- Interview your parents or grandparents and find out how they were taught to demonstrate respect to older people and people in authority.

Bulletin Board Ideas

- Put "RESPECT" in the middle of a large bulletin board. Around the word, put pictures or drawings of the different people students need to respect, such as parents, grandparents, teachers, each other, bus drivers, brothers and sisters, and others.

- Place the word "Respect" in large letters in the center of the board. Use lines to show that this word radiates to other words used to show respect, such as "may I?," "please," and "excuse me."

- Draw a U.S. flag on the bulletin board and add the words of the Pledge of Allegiance. Place student figures on each side of the flag with their hands over their hearts.

- Use a large poster representing the environment. Add the words "Reduce," "Reuse," and "Recycle" and show pictures of ways to do each. Use the header, "Do we respect our environment?"

NOTES

P o s i t i v e

Definition

> **Having a good outlook toward life; looking for the best in every situation**

Objective

Students will become more aware of how their attitudes affect their lives. They will also recognize the effects their attitudes can have on others.

Application to students' lives

Choosing a good attitude over a poor attitude can make the difference between learning and not learning.

A positive attitude will help students make progress toward long-term goals and can reduce stress.

Having a positive attitude reduces put-downs among students and improves their ability to deal with negative comments when they occur.

POSITIVE ATTITUDE: *Having a good outlook toward life; looking for the best in every situation*

Short Lessons

- Talk about what it means to have a positive attitude versus an "Attitude." This word has been glamorized in popular culture to mean something entirely different from a positive attitude. Discuss the differences.

- Have students "apply for a job" by writing an ad that describes themselves. Have them highlight their strong points and skills in the ad.

- Ask students to design a collage that describes themselves in a positive way, and have them share their collages with the class.

- Give students a list of positive words. Ask them to mark the words that describe themselves and then write a poem or short story about themselves using these words.

- Have students give a 3-minute presentation on themselves to the class. Encourage them to talk about people or things they feel positive about, such as their families, pets, friends, or hobbies.

- Go around the room and ask students to tell each other, "A positive thing about you is…" The person being described should only respond with "Thank you."

- Have each student draw an outline of his or her hand on a large sheet of paper. Tape the papers to their backs, and give them time to write positive comments on each other's papers. Display these on a bulletin board.

- Discuss attitudes that make a person a good employee, such as getting along with others, being flexible, taking instruction, being willing to work, being punctual, and following directions.

- Ask students to write a positive note to their parent or guardian. Mail these notes to their homes.

- Discuss sources of negative feelings. What situations make us have bad attitudes? How can we counteract these situations?

- FOR TEACHERS ONLY: Send a positive note home about each child, highlighting some of the positive attributes you've observed.

The greatest discovery of my generation is that a human being can alter his life by altering his attitude.

—William James

Student Assignments

- Make a list of all the positive things you say today. How many times do you "think positive" in one day?

- Prepare a collage about yourself using drawings or pictures cut from a magazine or newspaper. Sprinkle positive words that describe you around the collage. Include some of the positive words your friends and classmates use to describe you.

- Prepare a 3-minute talk about your strengths and skills. Practice this talk on your family members.

- Interview an older person in your family or neighborhood who you think of as a positive person. Ask them to give you 5 pointers for developing a positive attitude.

- Make a list of all the negative attitudes you catch yourself feeling today. Can you identify what causes most of your negative attitudes? What can you do to change how you react?

Bulletin Board Ideas

- Use a road map or set of road maps as the background. Put a large star in the center near the word "Attitude." Mark roads leading from the center to other cities identified with previously-learned character words. Use the header "A positive attitude is the starting point for all your journeys."

- Use background paper showing lots of people. Add the words "People can change their lives by changing their attitudes."

- Use a cut-out of a large key ring with many small keys and another cut-out of a single large key. Add the heading "Attitude is the key to happiness" or "Your attitude is the biggest key of all."

- Draw a figure of Charlie Brown licking an ice cream cone. Add the caption: "Life is like an ice cream cone. You have to lick it before it melts."

- Draw a flight of steps. Label each step with the character words already learned. Use the header "Steps to Positive Character."

- Use the header: "How to have a positive influence" followed by phrases such as "Be responsible," "Encourage others," and "Strive toward excellence."

NOTES

Initiative

Definition

Readiness to take the first steps in beginning a project or action

Objective

Students will recognize that it is up to them to take initiative for their education and success in life. They should be able to identify ways in which they can take initiative in having the kind of future they want.

Application to students' lives

Learning to take the initiative will help foster self-esteem and self-respect.

Learning that most great inventors and thinkers had to take initiative will help students find courage to take initiative on their own projects.

Taking initiative will help students appreciate their own personal power to accomplish goals in life.

INITIATIVE: *Readiness to take the first steps in beginning a project or action*

Short Lessons

- Tell students the story of the U.S. poet Maya Angelou and how she took the initiative to dramatically change her life for the better.

- Integrate the idea of initiative with problem-solving skills. Have students identify a problem where they could take initiative. Work with them to evaluate the problem systematically. 1) Identify the problem. 2) List all solutions. 3) List the consequences of each solution. 4) Choose the solution that best fits the goal.

- Pose several situations that students encounter and ask them to problem-solve these situations. Examples could include: "he/she hit me," "he/she stole my boyfriend/girlfriend," or "he/she was talking about my mother." Discuss ways in which students can show initiative when facing problems.

- As a class, write a letter to the editor of your local paper, stating the students' perspective on a problem in your community. Make sure the class proposes solutions to the problem.

- Have the class brainstorm new uses for everyday objects. How many uses does a spoon have? A table or chair?

- Discuss the word 'initiative.' What are the roots of this word?

- Talk about great ideas that people have had which have changed our lives from those of our grandparents—ideas such as computers, cars, electric current, and indoor plumbing. What kind of initiative was required to develop these inventions?

- Discuss the subject of "What I'd like to know is…" Have students brainstorm questions for which they'd like answers. Use these questions for a bulletin board.

- Talk about how persons who show initiative often have to overcome the pressure of others who say an idea won't work. Wilbur and Orville Wright are a good example. Discuss how the world would be different if we didn't have airplanes.

- Discuss opportunities that are available to your students to be involved in school programs and activities. Remind them that it takes initiative to try out or sign up for these programs.

Look at a day when you are supremely satisfied at the end. It's not a day when you lounge around doing nothing. It's when you've had everything to do, and you've done it.

—Margaret Thatcher

Student Assignments

- Take the initiative to help one younger student with homework. This could be a student at your school or a sibling, cousin, or neighbor.

- Write an essay about a problem (be creative) and an invention that would solve that problem.

- Write down five inventions that you would like to create. Pick one of those inventions to share with your class.

- Ask three different adults what device they would like to see invented.

- When you see a request for student involvement at home, at school or in your community, take the initiative and get involved.

Bulletin Board Ideas

- Show a neatly-dressed student with school supplies in hand. Use the heading "Character education is preparation for the future. Take the initiative! Learn character!"

- Draw a hot air balloon with students in its basket. Use the heading "Take the high road—Take initiative to develop your potential."

- Show several light bulbs emanating from a student's mind. Use the heading "Catch those great ideas. Don't let them get away!"

- Show a student at home taking care of flowers or baking cookies. Use the heading "Initiate something positive today!"

- Draw students in several scenarios, with positive scenes on one side of the board (friendships, good grades, flowers) and negative scenes on the other (such as fights, anger, poor grades). Use the heading "What did you initiate today?"

- Use the heading "What I'd like to know is…" followed by questions your students asked. Write each question with the student's name under it. Or, make up the questions yourself. (Some examples include, "Why does a cake rise in the oven?" "How do they get astronauts to the moon?" "How does a computer work?")

NOTES

P a t i e n t

Definition

Enduring calmly without complaining or losing self-control

Objective

Students will be able to distinguish behaviors that indicate patience or impatience and will develop strategies for being patient.

Application to students' lives

Students need to develop the ability to wait and to handle trying situations calmly.

Having patience helps students in their friendships and family relationships.

Patience is needed for school and work success.

PATIENT: *Enduring calmly without complaining or losing self-control*

Short Lessons

- Discuss the benefits of going to school for 12 or more years. Does it take patience to come to school day after day? What are the rewards of getting an education?

- Pose a series of situations where students could act with patience or impatience, such as waiting for the school bus or standing in the lunch line. Ask them to describe both types of responses. Help students develop a list of things to do when they feel impatient.

- Talk about the patience they need in school for learning a new way of doing math or a new language. How can they be patient with themselves as they learn?

- Ask students to write five sentences about persons responding patiently without using the word 'patient' or any variations of it.

- Ask students to describe a situation in which they were impatient and how it affected their day. What could they have done to be more patient?

- Talk about why it is so hard to be patient. Is it because we have other things we want to do? Is it because we have nothing to do when we're waiting? Develop a list of things to do when you have to wait for someone or something.

- Ask students if they have ever saved their money to buy something they really wanted. What was it? How long did it take? How did it feel when they finally got it?

- Collect a list of inventions that took years to develop. If possible, show slides or pictures of these inventions. Ask the students to guess how long each one took. Discuss the patience that was required to develop the inventions.

- Discuss what Benjamin Franklin meant when he said, "He that can have patience can have what he will."

- Role-play the non-verbal ways people communicate impatience. (Examples include biting nails, drumming fingers on a desk, or clicking a pen.) Do these actions cause other people to become impatient too?

Be patient with everyone, but above all with yourself.

—St. Francis de Sales

Student Assignments

• Write a paragraph about something you bought after saving your money for a while. How did it feel when you were waiting? Was it worth the wait?

• Interview a teacher, school leader, or business leader. Ask them how they have learned to be patient.

• Describe a situation in which you were patient. What did you do? How did your attitude affect the situation?

• Develop a plan for how you will respond when you feel impatient. Have a series of responses: first, second, and third actions to take when you are impatient.

• What types of things make you impatient? Do you do the same things to other persons that make you impatient with them? Write a paragraph answering these questions.

Bulletin Board Ideas

• Show a pastoral nature scene on the bulletin board. Use the heading "Adopt the pace of nature; her secret is patience." (The quote is from Ralph Waldo Emerson.)

• Use a picture of a Jack-in-the-Box holding a sign that says 'Patience.' Show other Jacks-in-the-Box who have fallen over or are broken. Use the heading, "Don't jump too fast. Be patient."

• Place a picture of a student in the middle of stacks of books and papers. Use the heading, "Hard work shows that you have patience."

• Have a drawing of a goofy-looking student. Use the heading, "Be patient with yourself—even Einstein had to do his homework."

NOTES

T o l e r a n t

Definition

Willing to accept persons and opinions that are different from your own

Objective

Students will be able to identify characteristics that show tolerance and intolerance. They will gain practice in seeing a given situation from another person's point of view.

Application to students' lives

Students must learn to get along with persons who are different from them in order to function well in our multi-cultural society.

Peer 'put-downs' are a big problem among middle-school students, leading to low self-esteem in many children. Learning to be tolerant will help reduce the use of put-downs.

Tolerance for siblings and family members will help students get along better with others in their homes.

Increased awareness of the tolerance and intolerance in themselves and in popular movies and TV shows may help reduce violence among children and young adults.

TOLERANT: *Willing to accept persons and opinions that are different from your own*

Short Lessons

- Discuss the statement by Aldous Huxley: "There is only one corner of the universe you can be certain of improving, and that is your own self."

- Bring in a newspaper or magazine article describing a problem in your community. Divide students into groups and ask them to discuss and then present one side of the problem or the other, or both.

- Teach students about the stages of anger, then ask them to write down examples of when they were at each stage. Discuss the role of intolerance in our anger.

- Identify a group or school conflict and discuss it in light of "I/I" or "Win/Win" statements.

- Identify a number of popular movies that show either violence or tolerance. Take an informal poll to see how many students have seen which movies. Discuss how our choices of entertainment affect our tolerance for others.

- Talk about the message of Martin Luther King, Jr. How did he think intolerance should be handled?

- Show the class a short clip from a cartoon. Count the number of violent acts in 10 minutes. Discuss whether the cartoon promotes violence or tolerance.

- Discuss the following quote by Martin Niemiller: "In Germany they came first for the communists and I didn't speak up because I wasn't a communist. Then they came for the Jews, and I didn't speak up because I wasn't a Jew. Then they came for the trade unionists, and I didn't speak up because I wasn't a trade unionist. Then they came for the Catholics, and I didn't speak up because I was a Protestant. Then they came for me, and by that time no one was left to speak up."

- Discuss the contributions made to our country by different ethnic groups. Ask students to identify the different cultural groups living in your area.

- Ask students whether they feel tolerant of persons with disabilities. How do we show tolerance and acceptance for these persons? Encourage students to practice being blindfolded and having to feel their way around or to watch the TV with no sound. How does it make them feel?

Though all society is founded on intolerance, all improvement is founded on tolerance.

—George Bernard Shaw

Student Assignments

• Bring in a newspaper or magazine article about a problem with intolerance in your community. Do you contribute to the problem?

• Identify an elderly or handicapped person in your neighborhood and help them with a chore or project. How does getting to know that person affect your tolerance for other persons like him or her?

• Keep a list of the number of times you put someone down in a day. Categorize the list by friends, non-friends, family members, and strangers. Who do you put down the most? How can you change that?

• Write a paragraph about how children learn to be violent. Do you think that watching violent shows contributes to the problem? What can you do to reduce violence in your neighborhood?

• A new kid has just started at your school. She wears very funny-looking clothes. Describe this situation from two different points of view.

Bulletin Board Ideas

• Draw a globe on large poster paper. Circle the globe with cut-outs of 'people figures' in different shapes and colors, with their arms or hands overlapping. Use the heading, "We're all the same on the inside."

• Write the word "Peace" in large letters across the board. Ask students to draw or bring in symbols that represent peace.

• Cut out figures of sailing ships of different sizes and colors. If possible, put students' pictures on each of the ships. Use the heading, "The same wind lifts all sails."

• Divide the board in half. On one side, put figures of people who are all the same color, shape and size. (Choose a neutral color, like green or blue.) On the other side of the board, use figures of people in different colors, shapes and sizes. Use the header, "Who needs a monochrome world?"

NOTES

Honest

Definition

Truthful; not lying, cheating, or stealing

Objective

Students will recognize the importance of telling the truth and be able to identify situations in which they have a choice to be honest or dishonest. They will also recognize the consequences of being dishonest.

Application to students' lives

Honest persons are more trustworthy, dependable, and valuable as future employees.

Learning to be honest encourages positive relationships.

Students need to realize that dishonesty has significant costs, both to them as individuals and to society as a whole.

HONEST: *Truthful; not lying, cheating, or stealing*

Short Lessons

- Give students a series of 10 scenarios in which they could choose to be honest or dishonest. Ask them to privately record what choices they would make in each situation. Collect the papers and give each student an "honesty" rating based on their choices. Return the papers to students at the next class.

- Play the song, "Honesty," recorded by Billy Joel. Divide the stanzas into sections (you may want to leave out some stanzas as inappropriate). Assign groups of students to discuss what each stanza means and present their interpretation to the class.

- Divide students into groups. Ask each group to create a 3-minute skit in which a person has a choice and either chooses to be honest or dishonest. Make sure students include the consequences of the choice in each skit.

- Discuss ways in which dishonesty in government affects the taxpayer. You could use examples of cheating on income taxes or larger political situations such as Watergate.

- Ask students to brainstorm times when they feel tempted to be dishonest. Divide those times by whether they involve family members, friends, or strangers. After you've discussed why students would be dishonest in those situations, turn the situations around so that the student is the one being lied to. How do they feel now?

- Discuss cheating on homework. What are the effects of not being honest in school?

- Brainstorm the many different ways there are to be dishonest. Help students distinguish between outright lying and dishonesty by omission.

- Calculate the dollar amount that shoplifting costs a typical store. Use real numbers from a local retailer, if possible. Then, calculate how much the storeowner would have to raise prices to compensate for what is lost due to shoplifting. Relate this to everyday items that a student would purchase, such as candy and sneakers.

- Ask students for examples from TV programs that make dishonesty seem glamorous. Can they recognize dishonesty even when it seems justified?

- Discuss with students why they often consider it an accomplishment to "get away with" cheating or stealing. Have them give examples of such situations, then ask them to identify who they injure with those actions.

- Discuss classroom disruptions. Do disruptions "steal" learning time from other students?

It wasn't until late in life that I discovered how easy it is to say: I don't know.

—Somerset Maugham

Student Assignments

- For one day, record the number of times that you are tempted to be dishonest. How many times were you dishonest? How many times did you choose to be honest? Did you have any consequences for being dishonest?

- Ask your parent or guardian if they can remember when someone in government was dishonest. How does your parent view that person? Write a paragraph describing the incident and your parent's reaction.

- Find an example in a newspaper or magazine of a person who was honest or dishonest. Write a paragraph about the situation and identify the honest choice and the dishonest choice. Explain what choice the person made and the consequences of that choice.

- Think of two examples from your own life when you were honest or dishonest. What were the consequences of your actions? How did you feel about those consequences?

- Write a short essay on one of these two topics: 1) What would a society be like if no one believed in honesty? What kinds of consequences would this cause? 2) What would a society be like if everyone was 100% honest? What kinds of consequences would this cause?

Bulletin Board Ideas

- Draw pictures of popular-style hats flying through the air. Label the hats with actions that demonstrate honesty, such as "return money you find," "tell the truth," "don't steal," and other examples that fit your students. Use the header, "Hats off to honest people."

- Use a picture of a traditional 'Uncle Sam' figure holding a sign. Use the header, "I Want You" and on the sign write "To Be Honest."

- Divide the board into sections. In each section, create a series of picture situations where a person could be honest or dishonest, such as seeing someone drop money from their pocket, having an opportunity to steal something from a store, or being asked a direct question by a parent. Use the header, "Make the right choice: Be honest."

- Show a picture of a student looking stumped. Use the header, "Are you honest enough to say, 'I don't know'?"

Creative

Definition

Using one's talents to produce something new

Objective

Students will be able to identify activities that are creative and will be able to make a new object from simple materials. They will also be able to write an imaginary story.

Application to students' lives

Creativity is an essential skill in being able to think of new ways to solve problems.

Creative projects encourage thinking skills and problem-solving while also helping to reduce stress and tension.

Students who are able to figure things out for themselves are more independent.

CREATIVE: *Using one's talents to produce something new*

Short Lessons

- Ask students to describe themselves using words that begin with the same letter as each initial of their names. (For example, someone with the initials AGK could describe himself as "Active, Gracious, Kind.") Encourage students to create several word combinations.

- Ask students to describe themselves using a different word for each letter of the alphabet (A to Z).

- Give students a set time period in which to write down all the words they can think of that start with the first letter of their first name. (You could also have them write down all the other boys' or girls' names, all the foods, all the games, etc., which begin with that letter.) At the end of the time period, ask them to count up the total number of words.

- Using a simple tool or a clock, take the object apart in front of the class and put it back together again. Show the students how to keep up with what they are doing; have the class help you by taking notes of the steps you take.

- Ask students where they think ideas come from. Help them realize that although ideas come from TV and videos, they also come when you are talking with friends and family, when you're walking outside, when you are simply thinking quietly. Point out that healthy eating, enough rest, and exercise can help a person be creative.

- Discuss excerpts from the book, *When Smart People Fail,* by Carol Hyatt and Linda Gottlieb. Use examples in this book to demonstrate how creative people can be in coping with failure and moving on to new experiences.

- Give groups of 2 or 3 students different topics related to your subject area and a limited amount of materials (perhaps only colored paper). Ask them to create a poster that represents that topic using only the materials you've provided. Display the posters in the classroom and, if possible, enter the posters in a contest.

- Ask students to plan a trip in a hot air balloon. Where would they go? What would they take with them? How long would they be gone?

- Prepare a transparency with only the words, "For me to be more creative I need to…" Ask students to create their own list to answer this question. (You may find it helpful to look at the list by the same name in *Chicken Soup for the Soul,* complied by Jack Canfield and Mark Hansen.)

- Have students brainstorm ways to be creative when doing homework assignments or chores at home. As you do this exercise, discuss the importance of not giving up if you don't know what to do. Who could they call when they are stumped?

- Help students design greeting cards to send to a friend, teacher, or parent. Provide paper supplies, rubber stamps, and stamp pads.

[Note: Another resource for teaching creativity is the book *All About Creativity*, by William Reid, Jr. (Walch Publishing).]

The mind is a bit like a garden. If it isn't fed and cultivated, weeds will take it over.

—Irving Hall

Student Assignments

- Write a poem about yourself that describes your personality. Use at least 6 different adjectives to describe yourself in the poem.

- Draw a picture of something in your home. The picture can be a landscape (such as your bedroom), a portrait (of your little sister, for example), or a still life (an object).

- Design a creative book cover for a textbook or a class report.

- Plan a trip in a hot air balloon. Where do you want to go? What route will you take to get there? What things will you take with you? Write a story about your imaginary trip.

- Choose a famous inventor and write a paragraph about their invention. Then write a paragraph about something you'd like to invent.

- Ask your parent or guardian to give you the first sentence of a story. Write a short story which begins with that sentence.

Bulletin Board Ideas

- Affix objects of different sizes, shapes, colors and functions to the bulletin board. (You could use real objects, such as construction paper in different shapes, large buttons, plastic gadgets, marking pens, etc., or you could use colorful pictures of objects from magazines.) Use the heading, "What can you create with a little *Imagination*?"

- Divide the board into sections, perhaps in wedges like a pie. In each section, include pictures from different areas such as baking, wood-working, singing, writing stories, or planting a garden. Use the header, "Where can you be creative today?"

- Put a large world figure on a background full of stars. Use the heading, "There are no limits to your creativity."

- Illustrate steps to creativity using a set of stairs with each step labeled, such as: Studying, Thinking, Designing, Working, Redesigning, Reworking, Trying Again. Use the header, "There's more than one step to being creative."

- Cover the board with pictures of healthy foods. Use the header, "Good food—the fuel for creativity!"

NOTES

Self-Respect

Definition

Taking pride in and caring for oneself

Objective

Students will be able to identify ways that self-respect benefits them, will develop strategies for developing self-respect, and will learn ways they can help others gain self-respect.

Application to students' lives

Learning to accept oneself and take pride in one's abilities is important to being happy and well-adjusted as an adult.

Students with a healthy self-respect are better able to resist peer pressure and be a positive influence on their peer group.

Students with self-respect will be less likely to engage in risky behaviors; they will also be less influenced by negative comments made to them by other students or siblings.

SELF-RESPECT: *Taking pride in and caring for oneself*

Short Lessons

- Present a list of characteristics that describe a person with self-respect, or develop this list with the students. Have students select the characteristics that apply to them and add other characteristics they think are appropriate.

- Prepare a self-profile sheet for students to complete. Ask them to list three each of the following: qualities they like best in themselves, qualities they think their teachers like, qualities their friends like, qualities that would make them good employees, qualities that their parents like, and hobbies or activities they enjoy and do well.

- Bring in a sack of small items that describe you, and introduce yourself to the class using these items.

- Show students the Food Pyramid and discuss the relationship between food choices and self-respect. Talk about the eating disorders anorexia and bulimia. How do these show a lack of self-respect? Discuss the physical consequences of these illnesses.

- Have students keep a record of their food choices and amount of sleep for one 24-hour period. Discuss which choices show self-respect and which do not.

- Ask students to draw a picture of themselves when they finish high school. In this drawing they should represent what kind of job they want to have, what their goals are for the future, what they will have already accomplished, and what their long-term dreams are.

- Have students make a list of 2 goals for the week and 5 goals for the school year. Collect the papers and write an encouraging note to each student.

- Talk about the differences between respect and self-respect. Ask students to remember the earlier lessons on respect. Are there any differences between these two character traits? What are the differences? What are the similarities?

- Discuss how our families affect our self-respect. Ask students to think of someone in their family histories who had a quality they admire and have them share with the class.

- Discuss prejudices and self-respect. Are these two attitudes related? Ask students to share examples of prejudices, then look at how these incidents affect self-respect—in both the person feeling the prejudice and the person receiving the prejudice.

Self-respect is the fruit of discipline; the sense of dignity grows with the ability to say no to oneself.

—Abraham Joshua Herschel

Student Assignments

- Design a word-poster about yourself. Put your name in the middle and use positive words to describe your personality and your future goals. See how many creative ways you can write the words.

- Make a list of three things you can do now that you could not do last year. What about five years ago? How much have you learned in this time?

- Ask your parent or guardian to write down five traits that describe you. Put that list in your class notebook and look at it when you are feeling down.

- Write an essay about yourself. Start every sentence with, "I like myself because…"

- Write a ten-sentence essay about yourself. Begin the sentences in the following way: I am, I think, I know, I wish, I feel, I wonder, I see, I believe, I can, I will.

- Draw a scene from your life with the heading, "I respect myself when I…" In this scene, show a time when you did something that gave you self-respect.

Bulletin Board Ideas

- Prepare cut-outs of student figures with the character words learned to date written across them. Use the header, "We are students of character."

- Cover the board with pictures of favorite sports figures in action. Use the header, "You can be who you want to be." Alternately, use a single sports figure who is well-known with the header, (for example) "Even the Shaq had to practice" or "Shaq *can* because he *thinks* he can."

- Show a beaver carrying wood from a tree toward his den. Use the header, "Build your self-respect."

- Display a picture of a student in a hot air balloon or hang-glider soaring above your town. Use the header, "I am somebody special."

NOTES

T h a n k f u l

Definition

Feeling and expressing gratitude

Objective

Students will be able to identify things in their lives for which they are thankful. They will express thankfulness to someone by writing a thank-you note.

Application to students' lives

Persons who are thankful for what they have are less likely to feel worthless or like the world owes them something.

Students who are thankful will be more appreciative of what their parents provide for them.

Being thankful encourages an attitude of happiness and generosity, and these attitudes are contagious.

Thankfulness is closely related to a positive attitude, and as students develop one they will develop the other.

THANKFUL: *Feeling and expressing gratitude*

Short Lessons

- Teach students how to write a thank-you note. Include a greeting, a statement of what they are thankful for, what effect the gift had/has on them, and a closing. Remind students that they can be thankful for kindness, or for someone who does a good job—thankfulness doesn't have to be tied to an object. Draft a practice thank-you note in class.

- Read aloud a poem about thankfulness. Give students a choice among several poems that represent thankfulness and let them earn extra credit if they memorize one of the poems during the week.

- Discuss the advantages of living in the United States compared to a third-world country. What about our country are students thankful for? Make a list on the chalkboard or overhead projector.

- Discuss being thankful for good health. Is good health something that students take for granted? Have any of your students had a serious illness or surgery? Do they have a parent or grandparent who is in poor health? How is that person's life affected by their poor health?

- Talk about being thankful for good food. Do your students feel thankful for the food they eat? Have any students ever been hungry, really hungry? What did that feel like?

- Discuss the kind of houses or apartments we have available in the U.S. Describe the shortage of housing in some countries, and how families have to share small apartments with other families. How would they feel if another family moved in with

them? Ask each student to identify one thing that they are thankful for about where they live.

- Discuss who 'deserves' our thanks. Is it important to say "thank you" to someone who is just doing what they are paid to do, such as the janitor, teacher, or cafeteria worker? Ask students to write a short thank you note to someone who works at the school. After you read the notes to make sure they are appropriate, deliver them for your students.

- Discuss physical disabilities. Do the students know anyone who is blind? How about someone in a wheelchair? Talk about activities that are challenging to a disabled person (such as taking a shower, answering the phone, or going to the movies). Do your students take these activities for granted? If possible, invite someone with a physical disability to speak to your class. Ask that person to talk about how they have learned to be thankful with a disability. What has that disability taught them?

- Ask students to bring in pictures or words that represent things they are thankful for. Make a class collage from all the images.

- Ask students to write and deliver a thank-you note to a parent or sibling. The following day, find out what kind of reactions they got when the person read the note.

A very interesting phenomenon in children is that gratitude or thankfulness comes relatively late in their young lives. They almost have to be taught it; if not, they are apt to grow up thinking that the world owes them a living.

—Fulton J. Sheens

Student Assignments

• Keep a record of how many times you say "thank you" in one day. Also keep track of how many persons you say this to.

• Collect pictures of things you are thankful for; bring these to class for a group project.

• Interview a person who came to the U.S. from another country; ask that person if they are thankful to be in the U.S. Write an essay based on your interview.

• Ask each member of your family to tell you three things they are thankful for, and make sure that each person says different things than the other persons. Don't forget to include young children in this exercise!

• Write a thank-you note to someone in your family who doesn't live with you, then mail your note to that person.

Bulletin Board Ideas

• Make a collage with images that the students bring to class. Put large letters spelling "Thankfulness" across the pictures.

• Cut out images of hearts that look like they are full and nearly bursting. Use the header, "Caution! Thankfulness can make your heart swell!" Alternatively, use images of smiley faces or smiling people and the header, "Warning! Thankfulness can lead to spontaneous smiling!"

• Show a large mirror reflecting a person's face. Place the mirror on stacks of books labeled along their spines with character traits learned to date. Use the header, "Can people see that you are thankful?"

• Place pictures of healthy food on the bulletin board. Use the header, "Are you thankful for good food?"

NOTES

Communication

Definition

> **Expressing your thoughts and ideas**

Objective

Students will learn how to express themselves using "I" messages. They will be able to identify roadblocks to good communication and will practice listening.

Application to students' lives

Students who can share their feelings with friends and family are likely to be less angry.

When students know how to listen to what is said, they are less likely to twist a message into something totally different.

By learning tools for effective communication, students develop refusal skills.

Persons who can communicate well are more valuable employees.

COMMUNICATION: *Expressing your thoughts and ideas*

Short Lessons

- Teach students how to give "I" messages. The sequence of such messages is: 1) "When you" 2) [Describe the situation] 3) "Then I" 4) [Explain the feeling]. For example, "When you talk about me behind my back, then I feel badly because I thought you were my friend." Role-play using similar situations.

- Teach students how to respond to criticism. Encourage them to be sensitive to the other person's feelings and to clarify the situation rather than responding defensively. For example, "I didn't mean to make you feel badly. When do you think I was talking about you behind your back?" Discuss about the importance of saying "I'm sorry." Have students role-play similar situations.

- Prepare a list of statements that students might make to each other. Re-write them as "I" statements. Respond effectively to critical statements. Discuss how misunderstandings can happen when we don't take time to clarify a situation or perception.

- Read from the book *How to Start a Conversation and Make Friends*, by Don Gaber. Choose excerpts and tips from the book and ask students to practice them.

- In groups, ask students to define a situation that irritates or annoys them and to work on how they can express their irritation in a constructive way. Then have each group present what they decided on to the class.

- Brainstorm roadblocks to good communication. For example, students may identify any of the following: ordering, threatening, preaching, judging, making fun of, cutting down, yelling.

- Invite a clown or mime artist to your class to demonstrate non-verbal communication skills. Alternatively, show a clip from "Marcel Marceau" or a silent movie. Ask students to identify the feelings or emotions shown in the clip. Discuss the role of non-verbal signals in our communication with each other.

- Have students write a letter to someone about an issue that is bothering them. Let the students know that they won't have to send this letter at all—but that writing down one's feelings is a good way to sort them out.

- Show different pictures from an art book or play clips from different kinds of music. Ask students to write down the feelings they have from that particular piece of art or type of music. Discuss how the sights and sounds around us communicate how we feel.

- Talk about how the clothes we wear are a form of communication. Do we make judgments about people based on the clothes they wear? Do we try to tell people about ourselves by the way we choose to dress? How important is this form of communication?

- Divide students into pairs. Have one student identify an emotion and have the other student express that emotion in their face or posture. Use such emotions as fear, anger, sorrow, happiness, excitement, fatigue.

- Play a tape recording of a passionate speech given by a national hero, such as Martin Luther King, Jr. What kinds of emotions do his words evoke? Why is it important that leaders be effective communicators?

Complain to one who can help you.

—Yugoslav Proverb

Student Assignments

- Develop a list of adjectives that could describe how you feel at a given moment. Try using one of these words instead of "OK" or "fine" when someone asks you how you are.

- Write a poem or song, or draw a picture, which reflects an emotion you have often. Share this with someone in your family.

- Start a conversation with someone you have never spoken to before. Write a paragraph about who you talked to and how it felt. Is it hard to talk to people you don't know?

- Practice listening to someone for 30 seconds. Is it hard to be quiet for that long?

- Interview someone in the class and write a paragraph about that person. Find out something you did not know about the person to report to the class, such as an unusual hobby or interest.

Bulletin Board Ideas

- Use pictures of faces showing a range of emotions. Add the header, "Express Yourself!"

- Draw pictures of students wearing different types of clothes and expressions. Label them with facetious names such as "Stay Away Sam," "Giggly Ginny," "Funky Fred," and "Dreamy Diane."

- Have a picture of a paint bucket or easel and paint brushes on the board. Use the header, "Do something creative—Compliment someone today."

- Keep up the collage students created in the lesson on "Thankful," and change the header to read, "So many things to be thankful for—Communicate them!"

NOTES

K i n d

Definition

> **Being nice to people around you**

Objective

Students will identify ways in which their words and actions affect others. They will practice returning kindness for unkindness.

Application to students' lives

Students will become more aware of other people's feelings in a given situation.

By thinking of kind acts and words, students learn empathy and respect for others.

Conflicts and fights can be avoided when students learn to react to a situation with kindness rather than anger.

KIND: *Being nice to people around you*

Short Lessons

- Have students brainstorm comments that have been made to them which are not kind, and list these on the board. Talk about how unkind acts make you feel.

- Make a similar list of positive, kind statements that students have heard. How do those feel? Is it easier to be kind or unkind? Why?

- In pairs, role-play different situations in which students are unkind to each other. Ask the recipient to prepare two responses, one returning unkindness and one being kind. Have the pairs perform this for the class. Talk about how issues can escalate when we respond angrily.

- Talk about whether it is easier to be kind to one person than another. Why do we have these prejudices? Do we carry grudges about things in the past, even from a long time ago?

- Discuss the old adage, "Sticks and stones may break my bones but words can never hurt me." Is this true? Have students give examples of how words can hurt.

- Discuss gossiping. What is gossiping? Is this a kind thing to do?

- Ask your students if they have seen the bumper sticker that reads, "Practice random acts of kindness." Do they agree with this idea? What would be a random act of kindness? Why would anyone want to do such a thing?

- Use the quote by the French author Pascal: "Kind words do not cost much, yet they accomplish much." What do kind words accomplish? Ask students to share a recent time when someone was kind to them, and describe what that kindness accomplished.

- Talk about how difficult it is to communicate with persons you don't like. Brainstorm a list of ways to think and speak kindly toward these persons.

- Place students in a circle. Whisper two sentences, full of details, to the person on your right. Have that person whisper the same sentences to the person on his or her right. Go around the circle until everyone has heard the tale. Is the statement that the last person heard anywhere close to the original statement? Talk about how gossip tends to distort the truth of a situation.

No act of kindness, no matter how small, is ever wasted.

—Aesop

Student Assignments

- Be kind to at least three people you would not normally be kind to. Watch for their reactions. Write two sentences each about what you did that was kind and how the person reacted. Add an introductory sentence to the beginning of your paragraph which explains the exercise.

- Watch for an unkind act. When you see one, interview the person who was the recipient. How did they feel? Describe the action to your class—without using any names.

- React to someone with kindness instead of anger when they treat you unkindly. How do they respond to you then? Does it make sense to return kindness for unkindness?

- Be kind to everyone in your family for one day. Does it make any difference in the family dynamics? Try it for three weeks—that's how long it takes to change a habit.

- Ask your parent or guardian for an example of kindness. What do they think is a kind thing to do for someone? Try to do the kind act they suggest.

Bulletin Board Ideas

- Put pictures of each class on the board, perhaps with different-colored paper behind each group. Add pictures of other school personnel, including teachers. Use the header, "We all need kindness!"

- Using large letters, spell out the following quote: "Three things in human life are important: The first is to BE KIND! The second is to BE KIND! The third is to BE KIND! —Henry James"

- Cut out a student-like figure with a large heart on his chest. Place a Band-Aid over the heart. Use the header, "Who says teasing never hurts?"

- Represent a field of flowers or a garden being tended by two student-figures, one male and one female. Give each student a watering can labeled as "Kindness." Use the header, "Kindness helps friendships grow."

Generous

Definition

Willing to share with others

Objective

Students will recognize that there are many ways to give to others and that generosity does not depend on money.

Application to students' lives

Learning to give to others encourages students to not be selfish.

Learning how to be generous helps students be more caring members of a family.

Students need to learn to appreciate generosity when it is shown to them.

Generosity among students creates a more caring learning environment.

GENEROUS: *Willing to share with others*

Short Lessons

- Invite someone from the United Way to speak to your class about what the United Way does and how it is funded. Ask the speaker to talk about the importance of volunteers to United Way programs.

- Using statistics provided by the United Way or other charitable organization in your area, design two charts related to where their money comes from and how it is spent.

- Conduct or participate in a canned food drive at your school. Point out to students that they don't need money to share what they have with others.

- Give each student an imaginary $100 and ask them to write a paragraph on what they would do with that money. Will they spend it all on themselves? Will they give some of it away?

- Brainstorm a list of ways in which the students could do something generous for their school. Point out that generosity can be a gift of money, time, or things.

- Participate in a coat, shoe, toy or eyeglasses drive in your region. Ask each student to bring in an item in good condition to donate to the drive. Invite a representative from the responsible organization to speak or write a letter to the class telling them where their donations went.

- Invite a person from the Red Cross to speak to your class about blood drives and organ donation. Why are these functions important? Discuss generosity in this context.

- Ask your students if they would like to adopt a child in another country. Figure out what it would cost to do this and make sure that your students are willing to bring in the money. Have the students write a letter to the child. Alternatively, you could ask the students to adopt a needy family for the holiday. Have the class talk about what they want to provide for that family and divide up the responsibilities. (You might check to make sure that the needy family does not have children at your school.)

- Brainstorm with the class the small ways they can be generous with their time and energy. For example, a student might choose to give up a 20-minute free period to volunteer in the school office.

- Share with the class how people like Booker T. Washington and Mother Teresa of Calcutta have contributed generously to the lives of others. (You can find stories about such people in numerous books at your library.)

It is well to give when asked, but it is better to give unasked, through understanding.

—Kahlil Gibran

Student Assignments

- Find out what the word "Philanthropist" means, and identify someone in your community who is a philanthropist. Write an essay about what that person has done.

- Identify a charitable organization that depends on generosity to stay in business and write a report on this group. What goods or services does it provide? Where does it get funding?

- Write a fiction story about a very greedy person. Cause something to happen in the story that changes this person's attitude.

- Choose a way to be generous with your time at home. Remember the definition of generous— willing to share. Report to the class on how you shared your time.

- Bring something to school to share with your friends. Be generous!

Bulletin Board Ideas

- Put a very large picture of a dollar bill on the board. Add the words, "Stretch yourself... Give generously!"

- Obtain flyers from the United Way and other charitable organizations in your area. Display these on the board along with the number of persons that each group helps in a year. Use the header, "These groups depend on your generosity."

- Place pictures of canned foods (or use actual labels), coats, eyeglasses, and toys on the board. Use the header, "There are many ways to be generous."

- If your class has adopted a child, display a picture of that child and an image of his or her country. Include any correspondence the class has received. Use the header, "Your generosity at work." You may want to adapt this idea if you adopt a family for the holidays. Then, the bulletin board could include a list of the items the class has decided to purchase and pictures of those items.

C h e e r f u l

Definition

Full of cheer, joyful, glad

Objective

Students will be able to identify cheerful attitudes and responses to situations and will recognize that they can choose to be cheerful.

Application to students' lives

Cheerfulness will help students have more fun in life.

Students may not realize that they can choose to be cheerful. Learning that these choices are ours to make can help students begin to take responsibility for their outlook on life.

Students with a sense of humor often have a greater self-esteem. Humor helps make the difficult times of life less somber.

CHEERFUL: *Full of cheer, joyful, glad*

Short Lessons

- Bring a *Reader's Digest* to class and read excerpts from the column, "Laughter, the Best Medicine." Ask students to bring in a funny story to share with the class.

- Tell students the story of Norman Cousins and how laughter helped him heal from an incurable disease. You can read his story in the book *Anatomy of an Illness*, by Norman Cousins.

- Talk about humor. What do we laugh at? Is it OK to laugh at people? Or should we only laugh at things or at situations?

- Teach the class a happy or silly song. Ask the class to teach it to one person at their home. Did that person like the song? Sing it every day for a few days.

- Have a day in which only positive statements are allowed in the class. (This includes your statements too, remember!) Stop when someone makes a grumpy remark and ask them to rephrase their remark in a cheerful way.

- Ask students to report on their interview of a person they know who is cheerful. What makes that person cheerful? Does that person have things to be grumpy about, too? Discuss whether they think cheerfulness is a choice.

- Play excerpts from several different kinds of music. Does one type make you feel more cheerful than another type? Discuss how the music we listen to can affect our moods.

- Have a "Laugh-In." During one class period, have each student bring in a funny joke or story to share with the class. Supply a few of your own. Use the time to talk about when it is appropriate to laugh and when it is not. Discuss how laughing at people is not cheerful (or kind) at all.

- Read the short story "Grumble Town," in *The Moral Compass*, by William Bennett. Discuss the benefits of being around cheerful people.

- Each day, greet students with a cheerful tone. Then one day, greet students with a grumpy voice and facial expression. Do the students notice a difference? Talk about how the tone of our voice, our body language, and our facial expressions can convey cheerfulness.

A cheerful giver does not count the cost of what he gives. His heart is set on pleasing and cheering him to whom the gift is given.

—Julian Norwick

Bulletin Board Ideas

• Use smiley face paper as the background. Add the words, "Of all the things you wear, your expression is the most important."

• Show a road leading from your school to high school to college to a workplace. Place student figures walking along the road. Use the header, "You can go miles with smiles." Use a smiley face for the letter "o."

• On cheerful-colored background paper, make a large circle out of letters that spell the words "thinking," "feeling," and "acting." Connect these words with arrows to indicate that one leads to the other in an endless loop. Use the header, "Think cheerful, act cheerful, feel cheerful."

• Draw examples of 10-15 different facial expressions and label them (grumpy, angry, bored, happy, tired, etc.). Use the header, "Do you wear a cheerful expression?"

• Show a large sun with rays of light extending from it. Use the header, "Let your light shine! Be cheerful!"

Student Assignments

• Write an essay on how different colored clothes affect your mood. For example, you could begin with "When I wear blue, I feel. . ." and go through all the colors that you wear. Do you choose your clothes to match your mood in the mornings?

• Interview the most cheerful person you know. Ask that person why they are cheerful. Write a paragraph about that person.

• Bring in a picture or cartoon showing someone who looks cheerful. Talk about what makes you cheerful.

• For one whole day, make only positive, cheerful statements. Is this hard to do? How many times did you slip and say something that wasn't cheerful?

• Collect funny poems, quotes, or clean jokes to share with the class.

NOTES

O p t i m i s t i c

Definition

Looking at the bright side of situations

Objective

Students will be able to identify optimistic responses to common situations and will be able to write ways to change pessimistic thinking into optimistic thinking.

Application to students' lives

Learning to change pessimism into optimism is a very important skill that can make a big difference in a person's outlook on life.

Optimism is closely related to self-confidence and success.

Students who are optimistic are more likely to be positive influences on their peers.

When students concentrate on turning negatives into positives, they become more aware of what they can accomplish in life.

OPTIMISTIC: *Looking at the bright side of situations*

Short Lessons

- Give students several hypothetical situations, such as a parent losing a job, a breakup between a boyfriend and girlfriend, or a house burning down. On the board, write a potential optimistic outcome and a potential pessimistic outcome for each situation. Does what we expect to happen have any influence on what actually happens?

- Ask students to write down and analyze the words from one of their favorite songs. Is the song optimistic or pessimistic? Why do they like the song? Discuss this assignment in class.

- Ask students to interpret this quote from Anne Frank: "I don't think of all the misery but of all the beauty that still remains." Remind students of the circumstances under which she was writing. Ask them to interpret the statement in light of the circumstances of their own lives.

- Play an excerpt from a political speech in which the leader was optimistic. Describe the occasion of the speech to the students. Ask them to identify what was causing the speaker to be optimistic.

- Bring in several ads from newspapers or magazines. With your students, analyze how advertisers use optimism and hope to encourage us to buy products. Does it work?

- Ask students to observe their behavior for a week and identify a time when they chose to be optimistic in a difficult situation. How did that choice affect the situation?

- Define the words "optimist" and "pessimist." Discuss how you feel when you are with each type of person.

- Invite a student to share an experience he or she has had in which life didn't "look good." How did optimistic thinking help the situation?

- Invite a soldier or veteran to share with the class on how they handle time away from their home and family. Ask this person to discuss optimism in the face of difficulty.

- Read the story "The Boy Who Brought Light Into a World of Darkness," which can be found in *The Moral Compass*, by William Bennett. Discuss the boy's optimism in a dark world.

Perpetual optimism is a force multiplier.

—Colin Powell

Student Assignments

• Write down and analyze the words from one of your favorite songs. Is the song optimistic or pessimistic? In your analysis, include the reasons why you like the song.

• Watch a news program tonight and count the number of optimistic news stories and the number of pessimistic new stories. Are there more of one kind than another?

• Interview an adult that you know. Ask what makes them optimistic, and what they do when they feel pessimistic. Write a report on the interview for class.

• Write a one-page essay about the most optimistic person you have ever met. What actions make you think of that person as an optimist?

• Prepare a list of "Top 10 Things That Make Me Optimistic."

Bulletin Board Ideas

• Divide the board into three vertical sections. On one side, show rain, thunderclouds, and umbrellas. On the other side, show sunshine and flowers. In the center, place the words, "When you believe in yourself, the sun is always shining."

• Use a picture of a giraffe with the header, "Stick your neck out: Be optimistic!"

• Create a display of a stormy scene with rainclouds and a rainbow. Use the header, "Are you looking for rain or rainbows?" Alternately, emphasize the rainbow and a pot of gold at its base. In the pot, place "coins" containing character words. Use the header, "Follow the rainbow to your pot of gold."

• Put smiley faces all over the board and the words, "If you're happy and you know it then your face will surely show it." Add the header, "Choose optimism. Smile at life!"

NOTES

Perseverance

Definition

Sticking to a purpose or aim

Objective

Students will learn the value of continued effort toward achieving goals. They will be able to share examples from history of people who have persevered.

Application to students' lives

Learning to stick with a goal until they achieve it will serve students well in getting their education and finding good jobs.

Students should know that all great accomplishments require perseverance.

Persons who persevere often learn to be patient with themselves and consistent in their plans; most success is gained through steady effort.

Perseverance helps students be better equipped to face problems in life and keep moving forward.

PERSEVERANCE: *Sticking to a purpose or aim*

Short Lessons

- Ask students for examples of perseverance from their lives. Do they have goals that require perseverance? Talk about the adage, "Nothing good ever comes easy." Is this true?

- Talk about perseverance in relationships. Do parents have to persevere with their children? Do couples and married people have to persevere in their relationships with each other? Do friends sometimes need perseverance?

- Tell students about Thomas Edison, who tried 1,000 different combinations before he found the right materials for the light bulb. (For a resource, use the book *The Wizard of Sound*, by Barbara Mitchell.) Talk about the importance of trying out an idea, sometimes over and over again. (Your middle-school students may give up easily if an idea doesn't work the first time.)

- Ask students to write down on a piece of paper all the things they think they can't accomplish in life. Run the papers through a paper shredder, or use the scissors to cut them up, and remind students that they can do anything they want to do if they are willing to persevere.

- Talk about great musicians and athletes. What does it take to become skilled at these activities?

- Invite a veteran to speak to the class on the perseverance he or she needed to train properly and be away at war.

- Brainstorm the different obstacles that can get in the way of our education. What can we do about these obstacles? Help students realize that financial and tutoring assistance are available so that anyone who really wants to go to college can do so, but they may need a lot of perseverance.

- Watch for a news program that illustrates perseverance, such as how citizens kept their town from flooding by piling up millions of sandbags. Discuss how perseverance can require much work but provide great benefits.

- Talk about the perseverance it took for Christopher Columbus to discover the New World. What are the 'new worlds' that we are trying to discover now?

- Ask students to watch for examples of persons who show enormous perseverance, such as a person injured in an accident who must learn to walk again, or a baby learning to walk for the first time. Discuss the rewards these persons will realize by persevering.

What lies behind us and what lies before us are tiny matters compared to what lies within us.

—Oliver Wendell Holmes

Student Assignments

- Interview a parent or other adult. What is an example from their lives when they had to persevere to achieve a goal? What was the goal? How long did it take? Write an essay describing the challenges they faced.

- Make a list of things you want to accomplish in your education. Then, make a list of what could get in the way of your goals. Think about how to avoid these obstacles.

- For one day, keep track of how many times you tell yourself you can't accomplish something because you're not smart enough, quick enough, funny enough, cute enough, or other. Try to reverse your thinking on these issues.

- Research and write an essay about a famous person who had to persevere to achieve a goal. What do you admire about this person?

- Develop a personal mission statement related to how you plan to persevere toward your goals.

Bulletin Board Ideas

- Have a picture of two people playing basketball or other sport. Use the header, "Give [your subject] your best shot. Persevere!" Alternately, use the header, "To win you've got to stay in the game."

- Have a picture of a person looking puzzled, with wadded-up paper overflowing from the wastebasket. Use the header, "If at first you don't succeed, try, try again!"

- Cover the board with images of graduation hats. Use the header, "You'll need this hat to be successful. Persevere in school."

- Display a classroom scene with students or cartoon characters. Use the header, "School. The more you go, the more you know."

- Place images of large rocks and boulders on the board leading up toward a sun shining at the top. Add figures of people climbing on the rocks. Use the header, "The rocks are what you climb on. Persevere!"

NOTES

A m b i t i o u s

Definition

Having a strong determination to accomplish a goal

Objective

Students will write long-term and short-term goals for themselves. They will be able to apply the term "ambition" to their own plans for the future.

Application to students' lives

Setting goals will help students realize that they are in charge of what they accomplish in life.

Students who have ambition are more likely to keep trying at school and work endeavors.

Having their ambitions clearly in mind helps students resist peer pressure to do things that are not in their best interest.

AMBITION: *Having a strong determination to accomplish a goal*

Short Lessons

- Ask students to think for two minutes about what "ambition" signifies to them. Write their ideas on the board.

- Discuss how four "A" attributes are related: Attitude, Attendance, Ambition, and Achievement. Divide students into four groups and ask them to develop ways to promote each "A" in their class.

- Assign students to write a 5-minute presentation on one of the "A"s. Ask a few students to share their presentations.

- Have students develop and present skits related to ambition. One person could be the one with an ambition; some students could act as supporters and other students could present obstacles. (This lesson can include the topic of perseverance as well.)

- Talk about goals. Why are they important? What are they for? Ask students, if we don't know where we're going, are we likely to get there?

- Read the poem by William Ernest Henley, "I Am the Master of My Fate." Discuss how each person determines their own ambition by choosing or not choosing.

- Read the story "Can't" by Edgar Guest, which can be found in *The Book of Virtues*, by William Bennett. Discuss how that word can hinder us from accomplishing a goal.

- Summarize *The Seven Habits of Highly Effective People*, by Steven Covey. Share these habits with your class and briefly describe how each habit can lead to accomplishing goals.

- Read the story, "Tommy's Bumper Sticker," in *Chicken Soup for the Soul*, by Jack Canfield and Mark Hansen. Talk about Tommy's ambition and perseverance to accomplish his goal.

- Inform students of services available in your local community to help people get ahead, such as tutoring programs and scholarships. Require them to write the phone numbers for information about these programs in their notebooks.

Intelligence without ambition is a bird without wings.

—C. Archie Danielson

Student Assignments

- Define your short term and long term goals, and the steps you need to take to accomplish them.

- Draw a staircase with several steps or use one provided by your teacher. Write one goal that is important to you at the top of the staircase, then write traits you will need to accomplish this goal on each of the steps. [Teachers: For this exercise you will need to provide the template of a staircase for students to complete.]

- Interview a parent, grandparent or other adult and ask them what ambition they had at your age. Did anything get in the way of that ambition?

- Write a 5-minute essay on either Attitude, Ambition, Attendance, or Achievement.

- Look for advertisements for community service agencies that can help people who want to be helped. Share your findings with the class.

Bulletin Board Ideas

- Put up posters of favorite athletes in action. Use the heading, "Know your potential… And break through it!"

- Show an airplane soaring above the clouds. Use the header, "Aim so high you'll never be bored."

- Show a race being run or some other sport requiring endurance. Use the header, "Challenge is the breakfast of champions!"

- Draw a set of monkey bars and label each rung with accomplishments, such as good grades, high school, college, good job, happy family, and others. Show a monkey swinging from the bars. Use the header, "Don't monkey around with your future. Know your goals!"

- Draw a large triangle on the board and inside of it place pictures of students doing various tasks. Use the header, "Try the Try-Angle when you face a challenge."

Courageous

Definition

The ability to face problems directly

Objective

Students will learn the difference between courage and risky behaviors. They will develop techniques to deal with fear and teasing.

Application to students' lives

Students must learn to distinguish between acts of courage and acts of foolishness. These may appear to them to be the same thing.

By gaining a new way of looking at courage, students will be better able to resist fights at school.

When students learn that trying new things takes courage, they may be more willing to try.

COURAGEOUS: *The ability to face problems directly*

Short Lessons

- Give students a list of situations. Have them decide which reactions are courageous and which are foolish. (Examples: Walking away from a fight vs. fighting, jumping off the roof vs. not jumping even if your friends call you "chicken," making fun of someone vs. standing up for someone)

- Talk about courageous acts that are required during times of war. If possible, show video clips of battlefield heroism or of persons hiding Jews during World War II. Have any of your students had a brush with death? Ask them to share how they felt.

- Bring in foods from a different culture to share with the class. As they are trying the foods, talk about how it takes courage to try something new that you've never eaten before

- Tell the story of Joan of Arc and the Trojan Horse. What did Joan do that was so heroic?

- Videotape a clip from the news about a person in your community who showed courage. Show it to the class and talk about what caused that person to be courageous.

- Talk about the courage required by the early settlers, pioneers, and immigrants who founded our country. Does it take courage even today to move to a new place? How many of your students have lived in other states or even other countries?

- Ask students to share what they found out when interviewing someone from another country.

- Talk about the clothes that students wear. Does it take courage to dress differently from the crowd? What do they think of people who dress differently?

- Read stories from your students about times when they were courageous. Ask students to guess which student wrote the story. Throw in your own story of courage.

- Talk about when we feel afraid. Have any of your students had to walk home alone late at night? Been alone in the house on a dark night? Discuss ways to feel courageous.

Courage is rightly esteemed the first of human qualities because... it is the quality that guarantees all others.

—Winston Churchill

Student Assignments

- Interview someone in the school or in your neighborhood who moved here from another country. What differences have they noticed? Write a paragraph about how that person had the courage to start a new life in your area.

- Write a poem or short story about courage. Develop a character who has to make a choice that requires courage. Remember that there are many forms of courage.

- Write a personal story about a time when you were courageous. Be sure to tell your teacher if your story is too personal to be read aloud in class.

- Imagine a world in which everything is different. (For example, maybe you got dropped onto an unknown planet from a Star Trek spaceship.) Write an essay about what you see. How do you feel? Imagine your courage as you explore this new world.

- Watch your favorite TV program and notice whether the characters are displaying courage, fear, or foolishness.

Bulletin Board Ideas

- Post students' poems and stories about courage. Use the header, "There are many ways to be courageous."

- Show a runner/swimmer/speed skater crossing the finish line. Use the header, "Do you have the courage to be a winner?"

- Attach many different masks to the bulletin board. Use the header, "Take off your mask. It takes courage to be real!!"

- Show several students circled around two boys fighting. Use the header, "It takes MORE courage to walk away." (You could also use the header, "A person who is big enough to push others around should be big enough not to.")

NOTES

Considerate

Definition

> **Thoughtful of other people's wants and feelings**

Objective

Students will be able to identify people and actions which are considerate and inconsiderate. They will demonstrate understanding of the term by using it appropriately in sentences and stories.

Application to students' lives

Students will become more aware of the needs of persons around them and thereby less self-centered.

By practicing simple courtesies such as helping someone with a heavy load or holding doors open, students gain self-respect and learn adult behaviors.

Increased consideration by and among students fosters a less competitive and more cooperative learning environment.

CONSIDERATE: *Thoughtful of other people's wants and feelings*

Short Lessons

- Provide students with a series of scenarios and ask them to choose which actions are considerate. What does it mean to be considerate? Why would we want to be that way?

- Brainstorm a list of ways to show consideration to others. Have students choose two ideas from the list to do when they go home.

- Take the above exercise further on a subsequent day, after students have had time to think about being considerate. As a group, identify a list of 10 ways to be considerate at school. Make another list of 10 ways to be considerate at home.

- Talk about how we can respond when people are inconsiderate of us. List possible responses on the board and then choose the most *considerate* of those responses. Suggest that whenever someone is inconsiderate of them, they use it as a reminder to be considerate of others.

- Find out what services are available in your community to provide support for persons in need. Talk about these services, and discuss how they show consideration on a community-wide scale. Is it appropriate that tax money be spent to help persons in need?

- Invite a recent graduate who is employed to speak to your class on the character traits they need to be successful on the job. Ask them to talk about considerations that they give and receive at work. Students will benefit from hearing real-life examples.

- Talk to your class about ways they can be considerate of teachers and other school staff members. See what kind of ideas they can come up with and share some of your own ideas.

- Prepare a class bulletin board using quotes that students create about consideration.

- As a class, write a thank-you note to someone in the school that the class thinks is always considerate.

- Read the short book *A Memory for Time*, by Leo Buscaglia. Talk about ways that students can be considerate of elderly persons in their families and communities.

Life is not so short but that there is always time for courtesy.

—Ralph Waldo Emerson

Student Assignments

- Write three examples of considerate actions.

- Send a thank-you note to someone who has been considerate of you.

- Go to a store near your house and notice whether the employees are considerate of customers or not. What actions do the employees do that are considerate? What actions are inconsiderate? Also notice how the customers treat the employees. Do we need to be considerate when we are the customer?

- Make up a quote about consideration that could be used on a bulletin board.

- Write an essay about the saying, "No man is an island, entire of it self; every man is a piece of the continent, a part of the main." (John Donne) What does this mean? How does it relate to being considerate of others?

Bulletin Board Ideas

- Create a bulletin board of quotes authored by your students. Be sure to give them credit just as you would a famous author.

- Use pictures of disabled persons being helped by others. Use the header, "Be considerate."

- Display an extra-large greeting card (i.e., bulletin-board-sized!) that begins with, "Thank you!" Have students write thank you notes on the card to friends, teachers, or parents.

- Show pictures of students picking up trash, holding the door, helping a teacher carry in boxes, and other considerate actions. Use the header, "The considerate students of [your school]."

Resourceful

Definition

Able to think of creative ways to do things

Objective

Students will be able to identify resources that are available to help them get an education. They will also begin to think of multiple ways to solve problems and apply a systematic approach to problem-solving.

Application to students' lives

Students who are aware of resources available to them at school and in the community can use these resources to help accomplish their goals.

Persons who know where to find assistance with problems are more likely to be optimistic and to try to make their lives better.

Resourceful students are more likely to reach the goals they set for themselves, both now and in the future.

RESOURCEFUL: *Able to think of creative ways to do things*

Short Lessons

- Divide students into small groups. Give each group a phone book and a series of "Where would you go for…" statements. Ask them to write several names and addresses of resources for the things you are looking for, such as: a karate class, a carpet cleaner, Chinese food, dry ice, or flute repair.

- Demonstrate the World Wide Web to your students, or have a computer teacher give a demonstration. Talk about the learning resources that are available on the Web.

- Ask a librarian to speak to the class about the resources available through the local public library. Have the students take notes on what is available, and give them a short quiz. Many libraries have music and videos for loan in addition to books; some libraries have quiet rooms for study or group projects. Other libraries have computers or type-writers available for use.

- Take a class trip to a vocational high school or technical school, or invite a speaker from one of those schools. Discuss the educational and training resources at that school.

- Tell students about school resources that are available to them, such as the media center, com-puter lab, counselors, school nurse, and psycholo-gist. Ask one or more of these personnel to speak to the class about their role in helping students and how to get an appointment.

- Ask students what kind of job they would like to have. Brainstorm all the resources they will need to get that job and where they can find job-hunting help.

- Discuss problem-solving techniques with students. Make a list of steps that they can use in a problem-solving exercise, and do a group exercise as practice. Be sure to make the first step "Identify the problem."

- Pose a series of questions to students in which they have to solve a problem using only a few re-sources. What would they do? (For example: Your homework falls behind the washer and dryer. These appliances sit too closely together to be moved. What can you use to get the homework?) Alternately, pose situations in which there are several ways to solve the problem. Ask students to list as many solutions as they can think of.

- Demonstrate a simple craft or gift that can be made at home with everyday materials. (For example, you could make a gift bag from a brown paper bag or from wrapping paper.)

- Ask students to think of ways in which elderly people can be a good resource. What kinds of things do they know that young people don't know?

- Invite a speaker from the local recycling board to speak to your class on how much trash is recycled in your community, or get some information and present it yourself. How many of your students recycle? Talk about how recycling is being resourceful.

Great things are done when men and mountains meet.
—William Blake

Student Assignments

- Using the goals that you have set in previous lessons, prepare a list of resources that could help you achieve those goals.

- Make a list of three resources from your school or public library that could help you pass proficiency tests.

- Make a toy or other craft out of throw-away materials, and be prepared to tell the class how you made it. What resource will you use to get ideas?

- Identify a problem that you've been wanting to solve. Write down the problem and the resources that could help you solve that problem. Develop a list of the steps you will take to solve the problem.

- Talk about what the saying means, "Children are our most important resource." In what way are children a resource for a community?

Bulletin Board Ideas

- Draw a large world on the bulletin board and place cut-out figures of students circling the globe. Use the header, "You are the world's greatest resource."

- Place a student figure in the middle of the board, and identify the many different learning resources available in your school using figures or shapes. Connect these resources to the student with dotted lines. Add the header, "We're here to help you learn. Be resourceful!"

- Represent the family aid resources available in the community using brochures or drawings. Include phone numbers and addresses in prominent letters. Use the header, "Help is out there if you need it."

- List resources that will help students on proficiency testing and where they can find those resources. Use the header, "Don't be afraid of proficiency… Be resourceful!"

- Display a number of gifts that can be made from household items. You might want to include the idea of gift certificates for washing the car, baby-sitting, or doing the dishes. Add the header, "Use your resources, not your money!"

- Show items that can be recycled and where recycle bins are located in the school. Use the header, "Don't waste our resources. Recycle!"

- Use different colors to spell out the following quote: "Do what you can, with what you have, where you are." (Theodore Roosevelt)

NOTES

L o y a l

Definition

Faithful to family, friends, or other commitments

Objective

Students will understand the meaning of the word and be able to identify persons to whom they are loyal. They will also see that loyalty can be applied to oneself or one's goals.

Application to students' lives

Developing a sense of personal loyalty fosters self-respect and encourages students to persevere in reaching their goals.

Loyalty can be used in a positive way, such as loyalty to a family or friends, or it can be used as a source of pressure, as in loyalty to a gang.

Knowledge and understanding of the school symbol and school song can evoke feelings of loyalty and generate school spirit.

LOYAL: *Faithful to family, friends, or other commitments*

Short Lessons

- Talk about what it means to be loyal. Who should we be loyal to above all others? Why is it important to think about being loyal to ourselves?

- Ask students to identify the persons in their lives they depend on to be loyal, such as friends, parents, siblings, and counselors. What does it mean to be loyal to another person? Make a list of loyal and disloyal behaviors.

- Recite the Pledge of Allegiance as a class. Discuss correct and incorrect ways to handle the flag. How does this show loyalty? What does it mean when the flag is at half-mast or upside-down? Are certain behaviors associated with loyalty? (For example, placing one's hand over one's heart)

- Learn the school song in class and sing it every day for a week. Talk about the school mascot. How did that image become the mascot for the school?

- Tell the story of how "The Star Spangled Banner" was written. Ask students to write a song or poem about their country.

- Talk about the consequences of loyalty. When is loyalty a dangerous thing?

- Discuss loyalty to a sports team. Are true fans only loyal when the team is winning, or does loyalty go beyond the winning season? Suggest to students that loyalty to family and friends works in the same way, but is more difficult.

- Use an example of a spy or other national traitor. Why are spies dangerous to national security? Talk about what it means to be a traitor. Have they ever been betrayed?

- Read the short story "Flag Day" from *The Book of Virtues*, by William Bennett. Discuss this seldom-mentioned holiday and why it was established.

- Talk about keeping your promises. Read a case study of someone who was not loyal and ask for the class's reaction.

We are here to help one another along life's journey.
—William J. Bennett

Student Assignments

- Write a poem or song about someone or a group of people you are loyal to. In the poem, describe why you are loyal.

- Memorize the National Anthem and the Pledge of Allegiance to recite in class.

- Write an essay about what it means for you to be loyal to yourself.

- Write the words of the school song inside your notebook. Draw the school logo or mascot.

- Write a thank-you note to someone who is loyal to you.

Bulletin Board Ideas

- Show a student with a list of goals, dreams, or ambitions (or figures representing these). Use the header, "Be loyal to yourself!"

- Display a flag and other national symbols such as the Statue of Liberty. Use the header, "We have a great country. Be loyal!"

- Draw a picture of a student playing basketball. Show the basketball, labeled with "Loyal," going into the basket. Use the header, "Aim for character." (You can use this bulletin board for several weeks, or put it up at different times, by changing the word on the basketball.)

- Enlarge the school symbol and define each part that is included in it.

NOTES

Dependable

Definition

> **Can be counted on to fulfill one's obligations and promises**

Objective

Students will learn that doing what they say they will do is an important part of being an adult. They will demonstrate understanding of this term by turning in homework assignments on time and being prepared for class.

Application to students' lives

Dependable persons are more likely to get and keep good jobs.

Developing dependability will help students reach their long-term and short-term goals.

Keeping appointments and commitments is important to success as an adult.

DEPENDABLE: *Can be counted on to fulfill one's obligations and promises*

Short Lessons

- Ask students to decide on one thing they will do every day for one week. At the end of the week, see how many students kept that commitment.

- Discuss the "American Work Ethic." What does this term mean? Have they heard about it?

- Brainstorm the many things we depend on. Divide the lesson into People and Events. In one lesson, have students list all the different people they depend on to get to school, such as a parent, the bus driver, and teachers. In another lesson, list all the events that they depend on to happen, such as the water coming out of the shower and the light coming on when you turn the switch.

- Talk about the ways in which students can be dependable, both at home and at school.

- Invite a meteorologist to speak to the class on how weather is predicted.

- Compare honesty and dependability. How are these words alike? How are they different?

- Develop a list of all the different words that could be used to describe a dependable person. (Teach students how to use a thesaurus to find synonyms.) Ask students to write a story about a dependable person using those words.

- Bring in a plant for the class to keep in the room. Ask for volunteers to water the plant, a different student each week. Talk about how plants and pets depend on us to keep our commitments to them.

- Define procrastination. Give students a short list of ways to manage their time on a big project, such as breaking the project into sections, doing a little bit each day, and taking advantage of times when they are waiting for something else.

- Talk with students about setting up a student mentoring program. Review the rules or guidelines for mentoring and stress the aspect of dependability.

There are no shortcuts to any place worth going.
—Beverly Sills

Student Assignments

- Interview a manager or supervisor you know or who works at a business in your neighborhood. (Be resourceful!) Ask them what kind of dependability they expect from their employees. What are the effects on the business if an employee is not dependable? What happens to that employee? Write a report on your interview.

- Make a chart of all the things that are expected of you in the next week. Check off when you have completed the tasks. Rate your dependability by how many tasks you get done on time and how many are late.

- Begin a private journal in which you write about your day and your feelings. Write in it every day or every other day, according to what you decide is reasonable.

- Get a houseplant to keep in your room. Notice how that plant depends on you for water.

- Make a commitment to tutor a younger student or sibling one day a week. See if you can stick with it for the rest of the school year.

Bulletin Board Ideas

- Show pictures of friends laughing, having fun together, or talking seriously. Use the header, "Are you a dependable friend?"

- Illustrate a calendar with appointments and assignments and a large clock. Use the header, "Be dependable. Plan your time."

- Show a student in the center of the board. To one side, have pictures of family, younger brothers and sisters, pets, and friends. To the other side, have pictures of family members, friends, teachers, and other school personnel. Use the headers, "Who is depending on you?" and "Who are you depending on?"

- Show a large globe and/or pictures of beautiful scenery. Use the heading, "The future depends on you!"

NOTES

Compassionate

Definition

Feeling for another's sorrow or hardship

Objective

Students will learn to recognize the needs and feelings of others. They will understand that compassion also relates to the fate of animals.

Application to students' lives

Compassionate students are less likely to be involved in gossip, name-calling, and other unkind behaviors typical among peers at the middle-school age.

Compassionate people are more likely to be sensitive to the needs of elderly persons, persons who are different from them, and animals; they are less likely to engage in inhumane treatment.

COMPASSIONATE: *Feeling for another's sorrow or hardship*

Short Lessons

- Bring in a newspaper clipping about someone in your community who has experienced a hardship. Ask students how it makes them feel to hear about this person. Do they feel like they want to help?

- Discuss the differences between compassion, pity, and sympathy. How are these terms alike? After distinguishing the meanings of these terms, ask students to write two sentences using each term.

- Read an excerpt from a piece of literature (your choice) and ask students to identify with a particular character. If they were involved in the scene, would they want to help that person?

- What is the opposite of compassion? Discuss how it feels to have a hardship and for others not to care. Have any students experienced this feeling?

- Prepare a short lesson on a person whose life was devoted to a compassionate cause. Talk about members of your community who your students think of as compassionate.

- Invite a family therapist or counselor to share their work with the class. Why do they feel compassionate for families who come to them for help?

- Ask each student to share one hardship or sorrow they have had to deal with; after each person shares, ask how many other students have had that same hardship.

- Invite a representative from your local humane society to speak to the class on what this organization does.

- Prepare role-plays of different situations in which students could respond with compassion. Teach them how to express themselves in these situations. (Middle-school students may feel compassion deeply but not know how to express it.)

- Make a list of things individual students and the class could do to demonstrate compassion for others in your community.

Make no judgments where you have no compassion.
—Anne McCaffrey

Student Assignments

- Find a newspaper or magazine article about an organization that cares for animals or for the environment. What can you learn about the organization from the article?

- Interview two persons who have been shown compassion. What were their experiences? Be prepared to share with your class.

- Volunteer for an afternoon at the local Humane Society, a homeless shelter or a food bank. Write an essay about how you felt when you were helping out.

- Look for three opportunities to show compassion this week. Record what made you feel compassionate and how you responded.

- Watch an "After-School Special" and write a short essay about the feelings you had related to the situation in the TV special.

Bulletin Board Ideas

- Use a picture of a globe with the header, "Improve your world—be compassionate!"

- Show a picture of the class or use snapshots of individuals in the class. Use the header, "We can make a difference in the world!"

- Show photos of different animals and persons, including the elderly, babies, young children, parents, teachers, and students. Use the header, "Who needs compassion? We all do."

- Fill the bulletin board with the newspaper clippings that students bring to class. Add the header, "Watch for opportunities to be compassionate."

NOTES

Citizenship

Definition

Carrying out the duties and responsibilities to one's country

Objective

Students will be able to identify national symbols and know how to act with respect to these symbols. They will be able to list duties and privileges of being a U.S. citizen.

Application to students' lives

Students who have developed a respect and regard for their citizenship are less likely to be involved in para-military and anti-government activities as adults.

Good citizens know that the ability to vote is a privilege to be taken seriously.

Good citizens are law-abiding.

GOOD CITIZENSHIP: *Carrying out the duties and responsibilities to one's country*

Short Lessons

- Review the Pledge of Allegiance and the National Anthem. Require students to memorize the words to these national sayings and to identify correct conduct during their recitation.

- Review how the U.S. flag should be handled. Discuss correct folding procedures and regulations about rain and national tragedy.

- Have a discussion about taxes. Is it the duty of citizens to pay their taxes? Brainstorm all the goods and services that taxes provide. (Students may be unaware of many of the ways taxes benefit everyone.)

- Compare the tax rate in the U.S. with the tax rate in other countries, versus the services provided. Which systems seem most fair?

- Design a worksheet on which students list duties of a good citizen and benefits of being a good citizen. What are we entitled to as citizens of the U.S.?

- Invite an armed services recruiter to speak to the class about career options in the military.

- Read "The American Creed," by William Tyler Page, which can be found in *The Book of Virtues*, by William Bennett. Ask students for their response.

- Sing the National Anthem together as a class.

- Discuss freedom of speech. Why is this a very important part of our country's identity?

- Share facts about our National Park System with students. Discuss the rights and responsibilities related to using these parks. Does it show good citizenship to leave trash or not put out campfires completely?

- Read the story, "The Stone in the Road," which can be found in *The Moral Compass*, by William Bennett. Discuss how actions, not complaints, often get a job done.

There can be no daily democracy without daily citizenship.

—Ralph Nader

Student Assignments

• Ask your parent or guardian how he or she feels about taxes. Do they think taxes are necessary? What percentage of their income goes to taxes? Write an essay about how the government could get money if it didn't have taxes.

• Write an essay on what your responsibilities are as a citizen of the U.S. This is a free country, but can you do anything you want?

• Memorize the Preamble to the Declaration of Independence.

• Write a paper about an American Hero. Why is this person a hero?

• Find a report in the newspaper about a project that is paid for by taxes. Does that project seem like a good use of taxpayer money?

Bulletin Board Ideas

• Show persons of all colors and nationalities spread across a diagram of the U.S. (Don't forget Hawaii and Alaska.) Use the header, "Liberty and Justice for All."

• Place pictures of famous Americans on the board with 'Uncle Sam' hats inverted over or under the portraits. Use the header, "Hats off to good citizens!"

• Cut out newspaper articles about persons in your community who are being good citizens. Use the header, "Meet the good citizens of [your town]."

• Enlarge a picture of the Statue of Liberty so that it fills the board. Use the header, "America: Land of the Free, Home of the Brave."

NOTES

R e l i a b l e

Definition

Can be counted on to do what is expected

Objective

Students will be able to identify ways to be reliable and will exhibit reliability by preparing homework assignments on time.

Application to students' lives

Reliable students become valuable employees because they know to be on time for work and to perform their jobs as expected.

Developing reliability increases interdependence among family members and helps prepare students for eventual parenthood.

RELIABLE: *Can be counted on to do what is expected*

Short Lessons

- Discuss persons in the school who are reliable. Talk about the guard who unlocks the door in the morning, or the bus drivers. What would happen if those persons weren't reliable?

- Brainstorm ways in which students can be reliable at school and at home. Do they expect their parents to be more reliable than they are willing to be?

- What do we mean when we say that certain things are reliable? For example, is your alarm clock reliable? Is your mother's car reliable? How do we feel when the things we own aren't reliable? Is this any different from how we feel when people aren't reliable?

- Bring in a newspaper clipping or magazine article about a reliable person. Talk about how such people are often the "unsung heroes" of an organization. Why is that so?

- Discuss the relationship between reliability and self-control. Do we rely on our parents to be even-tempered in an emergency? Do we ever use the word "reliable" in a negative sense?

- Discuss the quote from Benjamin Franklin: "Well done is better than well said." What does this have to do with being reliable?

- Talk about how we depend on our parents to be reliable. In what ways are our parents reliable? What can they rely on us for?

- What does it mean to say, "We have to stick together," or "We're all in this together?" Provide students with several scenarios in which survival depends on other people's reliability.

- Invite a local employer to speak to the class about the need for reliability in employees.

- Discuss what would happen (or what does happen) when there is a labor strike. For example, if the truckers went on strike, what would happen to the food in the grocery stores? How does such a strike affect us?

Effort only releases its reward after a person refuses to quit.
—Napoleon Hill

Student Assignments

- Write an article describing a time when you were reliable. Create a big headline. Write in the factual style of a newspaper.

- Make a list of things you can be relied on to do.

- Do all of your homework assignments and chores reliably this week. What does that mean?

- Draw a cartoon of what could happen if someone or something that you depend on is not reliable. Be creative!

- Write an essay about a person in your life who is reliable. This could be a parent, a grandparent, a friend, or even a pet. How does their reliability affect you?

Bulletin Board Ideas

- Show pictures of an alarm clock, the school bus, a car going down the street, dinner on the table, or other items. Use the header, "What are you relying on today?"

- Show pictures of students sitting in class, smiling with friends, doing homework and chores. Use the header, "Are you a reliable person?"

- Take photos of your students doing assignments or working at a responsibility they have assumed in the building. Use the header, "A Reliable Class."

- Illustrate a ladder or set of stairs, with each rung or step bearing a different character trait. Put "Reliable" at the top. Choose other traits that have been learned which relate to reliability, such as "Dependable" and "Responsible."

NOTES

E c o n o m i c a l

Definition

Showing wise use of money, resources, and time

Objective

Students will understand the dollar value of their possessions and will develop a plan for managing their money. They will also develop an appreciation for the high cost of vandalism.

\Application to students' lives

Understanding the costs associated with simple things like dinner and housing will increase students' appreciation for getting a good job.

Taking stock of one's possessions gives students a greater appreciation for how much they have.

Awareness of money management is important for staying out of debt as an adult.

ECONOMICAL: *Showing wise use of money, resources, and time*

Short Lessons

- Discuss how to construct a budget. Use a student's income and expenses as an easy example.

- Have students list all the things that parents need money for, and add in the items that students might overlook, such as health insurance or money for braces. Develop a typical household budget, using simple numbers. Talk about what happens when there is an emergency or an unexpected expense. Where does the money come from? Why is it important to have some money in savings?

- Show students how to comparison shop for groceries. Bring in the ads for one week and ask them where they would choose to shop, based on the ads. Talk about other factors that influence grocery-buying decisions.

- Ask students where they shop for clothes. Talk about differences in quality. Are name brands really better than non-name brand products? Bring in several examples to compare. Show students how to evaluate the quality of a shirt or a pair of socks.

- Watch several TV ads that are directed at teenagers. Teach students how to de-construct the ads. Raise the very pertinent question of, "Do you really need this?"

- Ask students for examples of vandalism. Discuss why people vandalize, and who ends up paying for damage to public places such as school property and parks. Estimate what it costs to repair a vandalized locker or park bench, accounting for labor and materials.

- As a group, inventory everything in the classroom. Using real numbers, have students calculate the price to replace the entire class contents, including desks, blackboards, windows, and chalk. Multiply this figure times the number of classrooms in your building.

- Discuss the Consumer Price Index. Show students where to find this index in a newspaper. Using old and new advertisements, show students how the prices of common items have gone up. Ask students how much candy bars cost now, and if they can remember when candy cost 25 cents. How long has that been?

- Give students a hypothetical amount of "prize" money, maybe $1000. Ask them to develop a "budget" for how they would use the money.

- Talk about playing the lottery. Add up how much money you would spend in a year if you bought only one ticket per week. Is this a good investment? What are the odds of winning? Give examples of how the odds of winning the lottery compare to the odds of other things happening, such as getting struck by lightning.

- Discuss the difference between being economical and being miserly. Is there a difference?

- Introduce the concept of supply and demand. Why is it that popular things cost more money than unpopular things? Ask students for examples of this.

- Ask students to bring in pictures of things they wish they had. As a group, determine which of these items are needs and which are desires. Use these pictures to construct a bulletin board.

Only a fool thinks price and value are the same.

—Antonio Machado

Student Assignments

- Itemize everything in your room and estimate how much it would cost to replace it all. Use catalogs to get accurate prices.

- Write down how much money you have, how much you have coming in each month, and how much you spend. Then, figure out where you spend the majority of your money. You may need to track your expenses for a few weeks to figure this out.

- Develop a plan for saving toward a goal that you have. How much money do you need to reach this goal? How many months will it take to get there? What are you willing to give up now in order to reach that goal?

- Cut out an ad from a magazine that is aimed at teenagers. Write an essay on how the ad is trying to convince you to buy the product. Decide whether you will buy the product, and state your reasons.

- Interview an older person in your neighborhood or family. Develop a list of common food items, such as bread, milk, candy, and other items, and how much those cost at the store. Ask the older person how much they paid for those items when they were your age.

- Comparison shop for a shirt or pair of shoes you want. Make a poster with the item and how much it costs at four different places.

Bulletin Board Ideas

- Separate pictures that students have brought in into *needs* versus *desires*. Use the header, "Economical Needs vs. Consumer Desires."

- Develop a flow chart of the large number of steps it takes for a single piece of clothing to reach a department store to be purchased by a student. Use an arrow or asterisk to indicate all the points at which the item could be purchased.

- Create a bulletin board out of ads for lotteries and sweepstakes. In large numbers, indicate the odds of winning. Use the header, "What are the odds of winning?"

- Show a large trash can surrounded by items that you see being wasted at your school, such as paper, pens, pencils, notebooks, and clothes. Put a dollar value on these items. Use the header, "How much money are you wasting?"

NOTES

Empathetic

Definition

Complete understanding of another's feelings

Objective

Students will become more alert to the needs of others around them and will identify ways to help others during times of trouble.

Application to students' lives

Development of empathy for others will help students feel less isolated or misunderstood.

Learning to view the world from another person's perspective will help students become less self-centered.

Learning to feel and express empathy will encourage kindness and could reduce violence among teens.

EMPATHETIC: *Complete understanding of another's feelings*

Short Lessons

- Develop a program for welcoming new students to the class. What is a new student likely to be feeling on the first few days of school? What can the class do to help him or her feel welcome? Set up a "buddy program" in which the buddy is a different person every day for two weeks.

- Discuss what it would be like to be in a wheelchair all the time or to be blind. Make a list of the feelings that such a person might have. Discuss things that you could do to show empathy for that person.

- Provide students with a scenario that could evoke empathy, such as a best friend having a house fire and losing everything. Ask students to write a paragraph pretending they are that friend. Have them write another paragraph stating what they would do to help.

- Watch an excerpt from a Charlie Brown movie. Do we have empathy for Charlie Brown? Why do we feel badly for him?

- Discuss how empathy can help with relationships. How do you feel when you are upset and your friend doesn't try to understand? Point out that communication is an important part of developing empathy.

- Give students a series of situations in which two people have differing opinions. An example could be the parent who says you must be home by 9:00 at night and the student who wants to stay out later. It will be easy to empathize with the student. Can they also understand the parent's feelings?

- Talk about empathy in relationship to physical appearance. Have we all had a "bad hair day"? Pimples? What can we do to empathize with each other when this happens?

- What happens when someone fails in a competition? (For example, drops the ball at a crucial point in the game, comes in second at a track meet, falls while cheerleading.) Do we 'boo' that person? How can we show empathy?

- Discuss what we can do when a friend experiences a death in the family. How can we respond with empathy? (You could discuss the stages of grief so that students would be more sensitive to how their friend might be responding.)

- Read the story "The Drover's Wife" by Henry Lawson, which can be found in *The Moral Compass*, by William Bennett. Discuss the struggles of this lone mother in the bush country of Australia.

Friendships multiply joys and divide griefs.

—Thomas Fuller

Student Assignments

- Write a note to a person who has experienced a hardship and empathize with them. If you don't know anyone to write about, use an imaginary situation. Remember, you can feel empathy for someone who is struggling in school or having a hard time with friends, too.

- Interview an older person in your family or neighborhood. Ask them to describe a time of hardship to you. Can you empathize with them? Write an essay about their experience, and tell the story from their point of view.

- Find two situations at home in which it is difficult for you to empathize with a parent or sibling. Describe those situations first from your point of view and then from the other person's point of view. Be as fair as you can. If you're really brave, show your interpretation to the person involved and see if they agree with you.

- Write a story in which you are in a foxhole during a war, with bullets flying over your head, or a story in which you just failed a test you studied hard for, or a story in which you've recently moved to a new neighborhood. How well can you empathize?

- Find an article in a newspaper or magazine about a person who has experienced a difficulty. Write a story about the situation as if you were that person.

Bulletin Board Ideas

- Display a large heart in the center of the board with the word "Empathy" on it. Draw lines from the heart to pictures of people, groups, or animals for which students might have empathy.

- Show a large kettle with bubbles coming out of it. Label the bubbles with character traits. Use the header, "Keep your character bubbling. Add empathy!"

- Use large letters to state, "E is for empathy. No one ever said it was Easy."

- Place the figure of a person horizontally across the board. Use figures of balloons with "empathy" written on them to "hold the person up." Lying on top of the person have lead weights labeled as "grief," "worry," "disappointment," "failure," and "sadness."

NOTES

J o y f u l

Definition

> **Showing happiness and optimism**

Objective

Students will be able to identify times in their lives when they have felt joyful. They will be able to identify things that help them be joyful.

Application to students' lives

The ability to take responsibility for one's own happiness is an important skill that can make the difference between a life of misery or a life of happiness.

Joyful persons are less likely to think of themselves as victims.

Developing a capacity for joy is related to achievement in reaching life goals.

JOYFUL: *Showing happiness and optimism*

Short Lessons

- Make a list of 10 things students can be joyful about, right here and now. Is it difficult to come up with 10 reasons for joy that don't depend on being somewhere else?

- Brainstorm a list of what things make you feel joyful. Create a list of 20 different things, and have students choose their top three items. Ask them to write these things in their notebooks so they can refer to them when they are feeling blue.

- Discuss whose responsibility it is to make us joyful. Can someone else do this for us, or does joy come from within ourselves?

- Talk about the life of Helen Keller. What obstacles did she have to overcome to be joyful? What obstacles do we have to overcome to be joyful?

- Read the story "Your Second Job," by Albert Schweitzer, which can be found in *The Moral Compass*, by William Bennett. Discuss ways we can open our eyes to see little things we can do to bring joy to others.

- Make a list of activities that could bring joy into someone else's life. Have students choose one that they can do immediately after school.

- Discuss the saying, "If life gives you lemons, make lemonade." Ask students for examples of how they've "made lemonade."

- Teach the class a happy song. Sing it together.

- Ask students to tell their favorite "Knock, Knock" jokes. Take 10 minutes to just laugh at the jokes.

- Make a transparency of one or several comic strips. Talk about why comics are always in the newspapers, and why people read them. Allow students to share comics that they like.

One should take good care not to grow too wise for so great a pleasure of life as laughter.

—Joseph Addison

Student Assignments

- Find an example in the newspaper of a person who "took lemons and made lemonade." Write a paragraph describing the situation and what the person did to find a joyful attitude. What was the outcome?

- Find someone you can do something for to lighten their load or to brighten their day.

- Choose a comic that you find especially funny. Bring it to class.

- Keep a running list of the things that make you happy this week. Write them down in your notebook as they occur.

- Make up a happy song with at least four rhymes. Don't worry if the song is silly.

Bulletin Board Ideas

- Show a pitcher of lemonade and some lemons. Use the header, "If life gives you lemons, make lemonade."

- Place the word "Joy" in the center of the board surrounded by and connected to images of different people, including students, parents, teachers, etc. Use the header, "Joy travels as fast as light!"

- Place the following in large letters: "Do the math. Happiness + Optimism = Joy"

- Cover the board with flowers and greenery. Use the header, "Spring forward with a joyful attitude."

G o o d   S p o r t

Definition

Treating opponents with fairness and courtesy

Objective

Students will be able to identify the conduct befitting a good sport. They will understand that being a good sport applies traits they have already learned to the area of competitive games.

Application to students' lives

Good sports are less likely to get into fights over games or team loyalties.

Being able to win and lose with dignity is important to developing self-esteem.

Being a "team player" is required in most business situations.

GOOD SPORT: *Treating opponents with fairness and courtesy*

Short Lessons

- Talk about the actions that define a good sport and develop a list of 10 characteristics of a good sport. Ask students if they have studied any of these traits earlier in the school year.

- Provide students with two examples of poor sportsmanship. Discuss possible alternatives for the behavior displayed in these incidents.

- Divide the students into groups and have each group make up a skit about a sports game of some kind. All of the character traits listed in class should be used or shown at least once.

- Discuss manners on the ball field. Do some manners apply and others not apply?

- Talk about how to behave during awards assemblies. When someone is getting an award, what is an appropriate way to act? Is it OK to laugh or make fun of the person for their accomplishment?

- Discuss ways in which a family is like a team. Is there a captain? A referee? Do you ever have time outs? Do the players get mad at each other?

- Ask students for examples of sportsmanship from their favorite athletes or TV programs. How do these people act? How does it affect them to see athletes being bad sports?

- Discuss ways in which the classroom is like a team. Do we have a class leader? Do we get mad at each other? How can we learn to be good sports in class?

- Play a short game as a class (your choice). Discuss the rules of the game and why following the rules is important. What does it mean to say, "It's not whether you win or lose, it's how you play the game?"

In our play we reveal the kind of people we are.

—Ovid

Student Assignments

- Design a poster about being a good sport.

- Watch a ball game and look for examples of good and bad sportsmanship. Write a paragraph describing one incident from the game. Describe the incident. Was the person being a good sport or a bad sport?

- Write an essay comparing a sports game (your choice) to life. What are the similarities? In what ways are they different? Do both have basic rules that must be followed?

- Make a list of 10 things you could do to be a good sport in your class and in your family.

Bulletin Board Ideas

- Use the entire board to represent a soccer field or basketball court. Use the header, "If you learn from losing, you'll be a winner."

- Display pictures of school teams. Use the header, "The good sports of [insert school name]!"

- Show students with various expressions leaving the baseball field. Use the header, "The good sport ALWAYS wins!"

- Use pictures of various sports activities and the words, "A good sport is… loyal, dependable, kind, tolerant, patient, and considerate."

NOTES

G r a c i o u s

Definition

> **Showing kindness or courtesy**

Objective

Students will understand what it means to be gracious and will identify actions that demonstrate graciousness.

Application to students' lives

A pleasant attitude is needed for success in many types of jobs.

Developing a sense of graciousness encourages students to pay attention to how they present themselves in social situations.

GRACIOUS: *Showing kindness or courtesy*

Short Lessons

- Talk about the term "gracious" and what it means. Explain the connotation of gentleness associated with graciousness. Relate graciousness to sportsmanship.

- Show a video clip of Jacqueline Kennedy giving a tour of the White House. Why do we think of her as a gracious woman?

- Discuss what actions cause you to refer to someone as a "gracious" host or hostess. How does that person make us feel as a guest? Make a list of several things students can do to make adult guests feel welcome at their home, such as hanging up coats, getting them something to drink, or having polite conversation.

- When we are visiting in someone else's home, how can we be gracious? Use examples such as not talking loudly, keeping our feet off the furniture, being careful with dishes, and thanking our host or hostess. Develop a checklist of things to do when we are a guest of someone else. (Include writing a thank-you note afterward.)

- Discuss how we respond when someone gives us an unexpected gift. Are we embarrassed? Surprised? What is a gracious response in this situation?

- Provide students with a sports situation that they can role-play. Have one student provide the bad sport response and another student provide a gracious response.

- Talk about the origin of the phrase, "Goodness Gracious!" Do your students know anyone who uses that phrase? What does it mean?

- Define cliques. Discuss with students how cliques are unkind and leave others out, how people in cliques often tease and make fun of others. Is this gracious behavior?

We love those people who give with humility, or who accept with ease.

—Freya Stark

Student Assignments

- Prepare an essay on the life of Jacqueline Kennedy. Why did she represent graciousness to an entire nation?

- Write a children's story about being gracious and share it with one of your younger siblings, cousins, or neighbors.

- Serve as 'host' or 'hostess' for a family meal. What actions will you take to be gracious?

- Draw a picture of yourself visiting at a friend's house. Indicate in the drawing that you have remembered to be a gracious guest.

- Write a short story about someone who is a bully. Describe how people who know him or her can help this person become more gracious.

Bulletin Board Ideas

- Write a checklist of things a student should do or not do when visiting in someone else's home. Use the header, "Be a gracious guest."

- Write a checklist of things a student should do to be a gracious host or hostess. Use the header, "Are you a gracious host/hostess?" (This bulletin board can be adapted and combined with the one listed above.)

- Show a dart board with an arrow in the bull's eye. Use the header, "You can't miss with manners. Be gracious!"

- Show two drama masks or faces of two people, one looking unkind and the other looking kind. Use the header, "Which represents you?"

NOTES

Trustworthy

Definition

Belief in the truthfulness and integrity of a person

Objective

Students will be able to identify actions that demonstrate trustworthiness and recognize situations that test this trait.

Application to students' lives

Trustworthiness is essential to maintaining long-term relationships.

Employees who are trustworthy are more valuable to their employers and more likely to enjoy career success.

Recognizing the trustworthiness of persons in their lives will help students appreciate those persons.

TRUSTWORTHY: *Belief in the truthfulness and integrity of a person*

Short Lessons

- Discuss the definition of trustworthy and link it to the previously-learned character traits of honesty, dependability, and loyalty.

- Brainstorm and develop a list of characteristics of a person who is trustworthy and a person who is not.

- Provide students with situations in which they are tempted to be untrustworthy and have them role-play different responses. Discuss the ramifications of the choices.

- Use well-known sports or entertainment figures to talk about how people get certain "reputations." Are reputations ever built on trustworthiness? What kind of reputations do the students want to have? Why are "bad" reputations more popular than "good" reputations? Can students get a reputation just because they are members of a certain family?

- Ask students to identify five persons in their lives who they think are trustworthy. What are the characteristics that make each of those persons trustworthy? How would they rate their own trustworthiness? How would their friends or parents rate it?

- Locate the latest statistics on marriage and divorce. Discuss these statistics and the importance of trust to long-term relationships.

- Discuss what it means to "give your word" that you will do something. Relate "trustworthiness" to the character trait "responsible."

- Invite a speaker from the Big Brother/Big Sister program to discuss the program with your students. Ask the speaker to emphasize the importance of trustworthiness to the success of this program and to discuss the characteristics of a good mentor. Provide information about how your students can become involved with this program if they are interested.

- Invite a speaker from the employment office to discuss with students the types of jobs available and the requirement that employees be trustworthy.

- Read the poem, "You Mustn't Quit" from *The Book of Virtues*, by William Bennett. Have each student write a short poem about trusting others.

The only way to make a man trustworthy is to trust him.
—Henry L. Stimson

Student Assignments

- Interview a couple who have been married for more than 10 years. Ask them what characteristics they think are important in helping them stay together. Write a report on your interview.

- Research your family name by interviewing family members or using other resources. See if you can find out its origin and meaning. Write a paragraph summarizing what you found.

- Develop a checklist for evaluating the trustworthiness of a person. What criteria would you use to evaluate this characteristic? (You may want to write down how a trustworthy person would respond in a series of situations.)

- Write a thank-you note to someone you think is trustworthy. In the note, give that person a specific example of why you think they are trustworthy.

- For two days, keep track of how many times you make promises and how many times you keep those promises. How trustworthy are you?

Bulletin Board Ideas

- On one side of the board use pictures representing parents, grandparents, siblings, and friends. On the other side, use a picture representing a student. Between the two sets draw a street with two-way traffic or arrows going in both directions. Use the header, "Trust is a two-way street."

- Use a figure representing a student and the header, "Are you trustworthy?"

- Create a check-list of the characteristics your students used to describe a trustworthy person. Add the header, "Choose friends that are trustworthy."

- Draw a large hand with a string tied around one finger. On the board list several items that students might be counted on to do, such as chores, homework, after-school jobs and projects, and counted on not to do, such as gossiping or spreading rumors. Use the header, "Remember to be trustworthy."

NOTES

C a r i n g

Definition

Concerned for the welfare of one's self and others

Objective

Students will be able to identify ways to express caring. They will understand that caring includes oneself.

Application to students' lives

Being helpful and concerned about others helps build students' sense of self-worth and connectedness.

Caring persons are less likely to tolerate violence against themselves, others, or property.

Having concern for others helps students be less self-centered.

Learning to care for themselves helps students become independent and responsible for their personal well-being.

CARING: *Concerned for the welfare of one's self and others*

Short Lessons

- Each day, choose a different person that students are likely to interact with, such as a friend, parent, grandparent, sibling, and teacher. Brainstorm ways to show caring to each of these persons. Have students choose one idea per person and do that as a homework assignment.

- Make a list of all the people students think care about them. What do those persons do to demonstrate caring? Is discipline a caring action?

- Discuss a classroom in which all the students care about each other. Post a life-sized outline of a student on the wall. Give each student an opportunity to write put-downs and derogatory comments they have heard on this student figure. Then roll up the poster and throw it away, telling students that you don't expect them to use those terms in your classroom.

- Ask students if there are any people they don't care about. Why don't they care about these persons? Identify the roots for uncaring attitudes, such as fear, prejudice, grudges, and jealousy. Remind students that we usually get back the same attitudes that we give out.

- Talk about the "language of caring." What words suggest a caring attitude? What words don't sound very caring? Make a list of caring words and phrases.

- As a class, decide on one thing you can do to show caring for your school or community. (This could mean collecting items for a donation, picking up trash in front of the school, or singing at a senior citizens center.) Do this activity together.

- Provide students with a series of scenarios in which a caring response is needed. Role-play various responses, identifying which ones are caring and why.

- Discuss ways in which we can care for ourselves. Ask students to list actions that show we care about ourselves. (This is a good opportunity to talk about staying away from drugs and other harmful substances.) Point out that "caring" is related to "self-respect" and "ambition."

- Ask students to share what happened when they did something caring. How did it make them feel to be caring?

- Discuss how we can show caring for the environment and for animals. Have students develop a list of ways to show caring toward the environment.

People want to know how much you care before they care how much you know.

—Unknown

Student Assignments

- Find a newspaper or magazine article about an act of caring. Write a paragraph summarizing the situation and how caring was shown. Would you have been caring in this situation?

- Do something caring. Report to your class what you chose to do, why you chose that action, and what the result was.

- Write a thank-you note to someone who was caring toward you. Either mail this note or deliver it in person.

- From the list you developed in class, choose one thing you can do to show caring toward yourself. Do that every day this week.

- Make an individual "Coat of Arms." Be sure to represent the people you care about in this symbol.

Bulletin Board Ideas

- Ask students for examples of "Random Acts of Kindness." Summarize these examples on geometric shapes of colorful paper and post them on the board. Use the header, "A Caring Class" or "Random Acts of Kindness and Caring."

- Display words or phrases that demonstrate caring. (If possible, use the same words that your students identified.) Add the header, "Use these caring words today!"

- Show a figure of a student or several individual students of different shapes and colors. Use the header, "Who cares about me? ME!"

- Post a large diagram of the Food Pyramid. Use the header, "Do you care enough about yourself to eat properly?"

NOTES

P o l i t e

Definition

Demonstrating good manners

Objective

Students will be able to perform simple courtesies, including introductions and taking of phone messages. They will understand good table manners.

Application to students' lives

Persons who are polite are more valuable employees than impolite persons.

Good phone and social skills help students feel less awkward interacting with adults who may visit or contact their home.

By learning good manners, students have a smoother transition to the world of business interactions.

POLITE: *Demonstrating good manners*

Short Lessons

- Place students in a circle. Going around the circle, ask students what they did fun yesterday. Note the responses as you go half-way around the circle. At the half-way point, introduce the word "polite" and its definition. Then continue around the circle with the question about fun. Determine whether the students changed their behavior after they understood that you were evaluating their politeness.

- Develop a list of small courtesies that a polite student would do, such as holding a door, helping pick up something that was dropped, or waiting patiently for a turn.

- Discuss good telephone manners. Have students role-play situations in which they both make and answer calls. Ask students to write out appropriate phrases in their notebooks.

- Discuss proper methods for making introductions. Ask students to play different roles and practice making introductions.

- Review lessons from the week in which you studied "Gracious." Ask students for examples of how they have been a gracious guest or a gracious host or hostess.

- Discuss students' behavior during plays, recitals, and assemblies. What kind of behavior is considered polite? What is impolite?

- Bring in enough dishes and eating utensils to create a formal place setting, or draw a diagram using an overhead projector. Teach students basic points about eating at a formal establishment, including which utensil to use with which course.

- Talk about verbal and non-verbal communication. How do we demonstrate politeness and good manners in our non-verbal actions? Use examples to role-play different situations.

- Discuss the quote, "The heart of politeness is respect." What does this mean? What does respect have to do with being polite?

- Discuss ways to interrupt or get people's attention without being impolite. Role-play common situations.

To have a respect for ourselves guides our morals; to have a deference for others governs our manners.

—Laurence Sterne

Student Assignments

- Invite a friend over to visit and introduce him or her to each of your family members. Practice being a gracious host or hostess.

- Write a short poem about being polite. What does a polite person do or say?

- Demonstrate that you know how to set a table by doing so at home. Bring a note from your parent or guardian saying that the table was set according to how you learned in class.

- For 24 hours, count the number of times you say "please" or "thank you" to someone. Are you being polite at home as well as away from home?

- Observe three persons at home, at school, or at work. Does body language say anything about politeness?

Bulletin Board Ideas

- Place blue and other colored award ribbons all over the board. Use the header, "Manners will make you a winner."

- Divide the board in half. On one side, represent a student at school; on the other side, represent a student at home. Use the header, "Good manners…" and the dual subheads, "Don't leave home without them" and "Don't go home without them."

- Place common words of courtesy (such as "Thank you" and "Please") on the board with the header, "Small words make a big difference. Be polite!"

- Show a building being built and bricks on the ground. Use the header, "Words are for building people up, not for tearing them down."

Cooperative

Definition	**Able to work with others to accomplish a task**

Objective

Students will learn fundamental tools for aiding group dynamics and will work together on a cooperative project.

Application to students' lives

The ability to work cooperatively is integral to family and job harmony.

Cooperative projects encourage learning from one's peer group and develop appreciation for the contributions of others.

Learning to compromise is an integral part of assuming adult responsibilities.

COOPERATIVE: *Able to work with others to accomplish a task*

Short Lessons

- Teach the class fundamentals of team dynamics, such as choosing a team leader, writing team rules, and encouraging discussion from all members. Practice these principles by writing classroom rules.

- Discuss how to handle differences of opinion among team members. Ask students for their suggestions, then provide a list of options for handling a disagreement among the team.

- Brainstorm and create a list of attitudes needed to work effectively on a team, such as accepting suggestions, being friendly, compromising, and not being bossy.

- Discuss the concept that "None of us is as smart as all of us." Is this true? Ask for examples of how cooperative effort has resulted in great discoveries.

- Give students a small cooperative project that can be completed in a short time period, such as building a tower of blocks or Legos™. At the end of the time allotted, discuss any problems that occurred when working together. Did one or two members take over the project? How were differences handled?

- Have students work in small groups to develop a poster about character education at your school. Allow the students to be as creative as they want using the materials you provide. As the groups are working, walk around providing instruction on how to make decisions and resolve differences as a team.

- Give students a more complex assignment to complete, such as writing a group story or doing a group research project. Encourage students to divide the task into sections and have each person responsible for a certain section. Give only a group grade on the project.

- Have students work together in small groups to write skits about the school year, their upcoming summer vacation, or the character education program. Provide a period of time each day to work on the skits, and have the groups perform for each other on the last day of school.

- Discuss the importance of cooperation in family life. Ask students for examples from their families of how cooperation is needed.

- Introduce the concept of cooperation on a global scale with a discussion of the United Nations. Bring this concept down to the level of local government, perhaps by discussing an issue of local relevance in which parties are divided on the best decision.

A single bracelet does not jingle.

—Congo Proverb

Student Assignments

- Work with your team to prepare a skit or story to share with the rest of the class. Do your part of the project with a good attitude. Take notes on the team dynamics —what's hard for you about being on a team?

- Interview an adult, asking them about cooperation on the job. What situations require cooperation in the business world? Write a paragraph about your interview.

- Look at the newspaper for an example of cooperation in politics. What is accomplished when politicians cooperate? What is accomplished when they don't cooperate?

- Identify five situations at home or with your friends where you can demonstrate cooperation. Is it easier to be cooperative in some situations than in others?

- Watch your favorite TV program. Write a short essay on how the actors cooperate or don't cooperate with each other. Give specific examples.

Bulletin Board Ideas

- Show a teacher fishing from a boat. Under the boat, list class projects on colorful paper cut to resemble fish. Use the header, "Gone fishing for good team work."

- Cover the board with pictures of groups of people working together on projects. Use the header, "Cooperation gets things done!"

- Show a large ring of keys; label each key as a different character trait and label the ring as "Cooperation." Use the header, "Cooperation: Linking the Keys of Character."

- Show a globe and cut-outs representing people from around the world. Link the people-figures around the outside of the world. Use the header, "Cooperation: Key to a Global Community."

NOTES

Ideas for Character-Oriented Bulletin Boards

- Draw a replica of the PAC-man or PAC-woman video game. Have PAC-man and PAC-woman figures, each labeled with character traits or goals, headed toward a sun labeled as "Your future." Use the heading, "PAC your life with good character."

- Show images of different types of school equipment with character words on them. Use the heading, "Have we got a fall for you!" or "[Name of your school]: A place to learn character."

- Show a large image of a student surrounded by character words written in different fonts and styles. Use the header, "Students at [your school] have character!"

- Use figures of male and female students with weights in their hands and character words on the weights around them. Use the header, "It takes practice to build strength of character."

- Show a figure of a lion roaring. Add the header, "We're wild about character at [your school]!"

- Use star figures all over the board, with a different character trait written on each star. Add the header, "Be a star! Shine with good character!"

- Illustrate the story of the "Three Little Pigs." Show houses made of straw and sticks such as bad habits, rudeness, and other negative traits. Prominently display a house made of bricks, with different character traits on each brick. Use the header, "Good character: Build your future on it!"

- Show a tree with all of the branches labeled with different character traits. Use the header, "The Tree of Good Character."

- Show a large pizza with many different wedge-shaped slices. Write "Character" on the pizza pan, and as a character trait is taught, add that word as a "slice" of the pizza. Use the header, "Grab a piz-za the action at [your school]."

- Show a picture of a student wearing graduation clothes and tipping his or her hat. Add the header, "Education: Don't leave school without it." Use the subheader, "Good character lasts a lifetime."

- Show a large magnifying glass and numerous character words such as 'polite, kind, gracious, courteous, respectful, thoughtful." Use the header, "Magnify your manners."

- Show a multi-colored flag with many stripes. Label each stripe with a different character trait and its definition. Add the header, "Are you flying the flag of character?"

NOTES

Suggested Resources for Teachers

Beane, Jim and Lipka, Dick. *When the Kids Come First. Enhancing Self-Esteem.* Columbus, OH: National Middle School Association, 1987.

Bennett, William L. *The Book of Virtues.* New York: Simon and Schuster, 1993.

Bennett, William L. *The Moral Compass.* New York: Simon and Schuster, 1995.

Brooks, David, and Goble, Frank G. *The Case for Character Education. (The Role of the School in Teaching Values and Virtues.)* Northridge, CA: Prelude Press, 1994.

Buscaglia, Leo. *Personhood.* New York: Fawcett Columbine, 1978.

Canfield, Jack and Hansen, Mark Victor. *Chicken Soup for the Soul.* Deerfield Beach, FL: Health Communications, 1993.

Canfield, Jack and Hansen, Mark Victor. *A Second Helping of Chicken Soup for the Soul.* Deerfield Beach, FL: Health Communications, 1995.

Charney, Ruth Sidney. *Teaching Children to Care. Management in the Responsive Classroom.* Pittsfield, MA: Northeast Ohio Foundation for Children, 1991.

Covey, Stephen. *The Seven Habits of Highly Effective People.* New York: Simon and Schuster, 1989.

Faber, Adele and Elaine Mazlish. *How to Talk So Kids Will Listen and Listen So Kids Will Talk.* New York: Avon Books, 1980.

Huggins, Pat. *Helping Kids Handle Anger. Teaching Self Control.* Mercer Island, WA: Assist (A Validated Washington State Innovative Education Program), 1988.

Lankford, David and McKay, Linda. *License to Lead. A Middle Level Curriculum that Develops Awareness of Positive Leadership and Decision Making in the School and Community.* Reston, VA: NAASP, 1996.

Lewis, Barbara. *The Kid's Guide to Service Projects.* Minneapolis, MN: Studio 4, 1997.

Lickona, Thomas. *Educating for Character. How our Schools Can Teach Respect and Responsibility.* New York: Bantam Books, 1991.

McGee-Cooper, Ann. *You Don't Have to Go Home From Work Exhausted. A Program to Bring Joy, Energy, and Balance to Your Life.* New York: Bantam Books, 1992.

McWilliams, Peter. *Life 101.* Los Angeles: Prelude Press, 1994.

Nelsen, Jane. *Positive Discipline.* New York: Ballantine Books, 1987.

Vincent, Philip Fitch. *Developing Character in Students.* Chapel Hill, NC: New View Publications, 1995.

NOTES

Teacher Feedback Form

Your feedback will be very helpful in improving this manual. Please take a few minutes to share with us what you found helpful. We would appreciate hearing about any ideas that have worked particularly well at your school. Send completed survey to: Anne Dotson, P.O. Box 39314, North Ridgeville, OH 44039.

1.　In your opinion, how useful are the ideas in this manual? (Circle a number.)

(Extremely useful)　5　4　3　2　1　(Not useful at all)

2.　What did you find most helpful about this manual?

3.　What did you find least helpful about this manual?

4.　What does this manual need that it doesn't have?

5.　Do you have any other suggestions for ways in which we could improve this manual?

Thank you for contributing to continuous improvement in character education.

About the Authors

Anne Dotson has over 20 years' experience in public school teaching, much of that in middle-school grades. She has taught Computers, Family and Consumer Science, Life Skills Programs, and Quest. She has worked in volunteer positions as a youth leader and youth teacher for over 30 years. Recently, Anne helped establish the Character Education program at Wilbur Wright Middle School in Cleveland, Ohio, by serving as Chair of the Character Education Committee.

Karen Dotson is a professional writer with many years' experience as a youth and peer leader. She has worked as a quality control engineer, an analytical chemist, and a health and science reporter. Karen spent several years teaching problem-solving, team facilitation, and group leadership to adults in various industries. She lives in the San Francisco Bay Area of California.